Corporate Acquisitions and Mergers in Vietnam

Corporate Acquisitions and Mergers in Vietnam

Fifth Edition

Tony Foster

Bui Thanh Tien

This book was originally published as a chapter in Corporate Acquisitions and Mergers.

General Editor: Peter Begg

Wolters Kluwer

Published by:
Kluwer Law International B.V.
PO Box 316
2400 AH Alphen aan den Rijn
The Netherlands
E-mail: lrs-sales@wolterskluwer.com
Website: www.wolterskluwer.com/en/solutions/kluwerlawinternational

Sold and distributed by:
Wolters Kluwer Legal & Regulatory U.S.
920 Links Avenue
Landisville, PA 17538
United States of America
E-mail: customer.service@wolterskluwer.com

ISBN 978-94-035-4537-0

e-Book: ISBN 978-94-035-4547-9
web-PDF: ISBN 978-94-035-4557-8

Contents

Freshfields Bruckhaus Deringer

Freshfields Bruckhaus Deringer is one of the world's largest international law firms and also one of the most prominent firms in Vietnam. The firm received office licences right after Vietnam opened to the world in 1994. With offices in Hanoi and Ho Chi Minh City, Freshfields has been at the forefront of the country's economic transformation. The firm focuses its Vietnam practice on corporate mergers and acquisitions and has acted on many of the market's landmark transactions in the last decade.

Authors

Tony Foster is the Managing Partner of Freshfields Bruckhaus Deringer's Hanoi and HCMC offices. Tony established the firm's Vietnam offices in 1994 and has lived and practised in Hanoi ever since, giving him an unparalleled experience and knowledge of business in Vietnam. He draws on this to assist clients in resolving the complex issues that often arise in doing business in the country, whether originating in the vagueness inherent in Vietnamese legislation or otherwise. Tony is responsible for the work of Freshfields' Vietnamese and foreign lawyers whose legal and practical knowledge – combined with international quality standards – produces one of the best legal teams in the country. Tony and the team have acted for global companies on many of the most significant corporate, M&A and equitisation transactions in Vietnam. Tony was the first foreign lawyer to be awarded a medal by the Vietnamese Ministry of Justice, has been recognised for many years by numerous legal surveys as being at the top of the profession in Vietnam, and – in the most recent survey – is in his own separate 'star' category above other leading lawyers in the country.

Bui Thanh Tien has been practising law in HCMC since 1998 and has been with the firm since 2001. Tien is the partner and head of Freshfields' Ho Chi Minh City Office. Tien is the first-ever Vietnamese lawyer elected to the Freshfields' International partnership. He focuses his practice on private equity, M&A and inward investment. Tien spends substantial time acting for private equity investors and investment banks on their investments and divestments in the country. Tien either takes the lead or is involved in all of the complex corporate/M&A and private equity work in the firm's Vietnam offices. Tien has been recognised as a top-tier Vietnam corporate lawyer by various legal publications.

1 ECONOMIC, POLITICAL AND CULTURAL BACKGROUND

1.1 Overview of Vietnam's Economy

[01] Vietnam's economy has been developing rapidly since the end of the US embargo in 1994. Vietnam moved from a centrally planned economy in 1994[1] to what was called (within official circles in Vietnam) a 'socialist-oriented market economy'. The Communist Party, which runs the country, now accepts that economic development will come from the private sector. The fifth plenary meeting of the twelfth Party Central Committee of the Communist Party in May 2017 resolved to 'develop the *private economy* into an important driving force of the socialist-oriented market economy'. This resolution has been carried through into, and strengthened by, the Socio-Economic Development for 2021–2030 adopted by the 13th National Party Congress in early 2021.

[02] Vietnam continues to reform its economy with a view to industrialising and modernising the country and turning it into an industrial upper-middle-income country by 2030. In this process, private companies and state-owned enterprises (***SOEs***) are considered to be the key driving forces, with foreign-invested companies serving an important breakthrough role.[2] Accordingly, Vietnam continues to attract foreign investment, with a greater desire now to improve the quality of such investment, focusing especially on high-technology, supply chains and value chains.[3]

[03] Vietnam is well integrated into the world economy. In addition to being a WTO member, it has signed 15 Free Trade Agreements (***FTA***) and is negotiating a number of other FTAs. Most recently, the country has entered into, and ratified, an FTA with the European Union (which took effect on 1 August 2020), the Comprehensive and Progressive Agreement for Trans-Pacific Partnership (***CPTPP***) (which came into force on 14 January 2019), an FTA with the United Kingdom (which took effect on 1 May 2021),[4] and the Regional Comprehensive Economic Partnership (***RCEP***), an FTA between ASEAN countries and five other key partners of the region (Australia, China, Japan, South Korea, and New Zealand) (which came into effect on 1 January 2022), that also provides common rules and synchronises all of the relevant FTAs.

1 Visitors to Hanoi do not have to look very hard to find a huge statue of Lenin on one of the main boulevards.

2 Resolution No. 29-NQ/TW of the Party Central Committee dated 17 Nov. 2022 on fostering the industrialisation and modernisation process until 2030 with the vision to 2045 (***Resolution 29***).

3 Resolution No. 50-NQ/TW of the Party Central Committee dated 20 Aug. 2019 on foreign investment until 2030.

4 https://trungtamwto.vn/thong-ke/12065-tong-hop-cac-fta-cua-viet-nam-tinh-den-thang-112018; date of access: 22 Jul. 2023.

[04] Vietnam has the fourth-largest GDP in South-East Asia. Economic growth between 1991 and 2022 exceeded 7% a year.[5] In 2022, Vietnam's economy grew 8.02%, the fastest annual pace since 1997, backed by strong domestic retail sales and exports. Having faced external and internal headwinds in early 2023, Vietnam is expected to achieve a growth rate of 4.7% in 2023 and pick up again in the following years.[6] The Party targets GDP growth for 2021–2030 at 7% a year. Per capita income by 2030 is expected to be USD7 500.[7]

[05] Between 2008 and 2011, the Vietnamese Dong, a managed currency, was devalued by around 20%. Its value remained relatively stable between 2011 and 2014. In 2015, the State Bank of Vietnam (***SBV***) devalued the nation's currency three times, by 1% each time, and tripled the USD/VND trading band to 3% in a bid to keep local exports competitive following the appreciation of the USD and the depreciation of the Chinese Yuan. The days of a depreciating currency appear to have ended. At the beginning of 2016, the SBV changed to using a rate-setting methodology. Instead of sporadic adjustments, it now calculates and announces a daily reference rate based on a weighted average of Dong prices in the interbank market from the previous trading day. In 2022 and early 2023, despite the significant depreciation of local currencies against the US Dollar in most Asian countries, the SBV intervened and introduced certain measures to control foreign exchange rates such that the Vietnamese Dong appreciated slightly against the US Dollar.

[06] Vietnam has increased trade, growing both exports and imports into double digits in the last several decades. From a country that ran a trade deficit with the rest of the world, Vietnam hit a record trade surplus of USD11.2 bn in 2022.[8] In the first six months of 2023, both imports and exports weakened, but the country's balance of trade was still in surplus.

[07] Vietnam has a population of around 100 m[9] (the 15th most populous country in the world), which is still growing rapidly. Its young, hard-working and literate labour force is one of the country's competitive advantages.

[08] The Party has an ambitious goal to turn Vietnam into a developed, high-income country by 2045.[10] To achieve this goal, Vietnam will need to implement substantial policy improvements, particularly in infrastructure, finance, environment, and digital transformation. Based on recent history, it will do so.

---

[5] Data retrieved from https://data.worldbank.org/indicator/NY.GDP.MKTP.KD.ZG?locations=VN on 20 Jul. 2023.

[6] https://www.imf.org/en/News/Articles/2023/06/29/pr23247-vietnam-imf-staff-completes-2023-art-iv-mission; date of access: 20 Jul. 2023.

[7] Item II.3 of Resolution 29.

[8] https://www.gso.gov.vn/du-lieu-va-so-lieu-thong-ke/2023/01/no-luc-phuc-hoi-xuat-nhap-khau-nam-2022-lap-ky-luc-moi/.

[9] https://vietnam.unfpa.org/en/news/information-for-media-viet-nams-population-reach-100-million-2023.

[10] Item II.4 of Resolution 29.

1.2 Economic Integration

[09] From an isolated country that was subject to an embargo led by the United States until 1994, Vietnam has turned into a country with an economy well integrated into that of the world. Vietnam's first major step after the lifting of the United States embargo was to become a member of the Association of Southeast Asian Nations (***ASEAN***), and the ASEAN Free Trade Area (***AFTA***), in 1995.

[10] The second breakthrough was the ratification of the United States-Vietnam Bilateral Trade Agreement in 2001. This agreement covered not only trade in goods but also trade in services, intellectual property rights and other investment-related issues. It committed Vietnam to a number of trade-related reforms, with the United States granting Most Favoured Nation status to Vietnamese imports.

[11] The full integration of Vietnam into the multilateral trade system occurred with its accession to the World Trade Organisation (***WTO***) on 11 January 2007. Vietnam is now a party to all major WTO agreements, including the General Agreement on Trade in Services, the Agreement on Trade-Related Aspects of Intellectual Property Rights and the Agreement on Trade-Related Investment Measures.

[12] On 4 February 2016, Vietnam entered into the TPP Agreement with Australia, Brunei, Canada, Chile, Japan, Malaysia, Mexico, New Zealand, Peru, Singapore and the United States. After the United States withdrew, the remaining nations signed a new trade agreement with an unwieldy name, the Comprehensive and Progressive Agreement for Trans-Pacific Partnership (***CPTPP***), incorporating most of the provisions of the TPP. Ratified by Vietnam in November 2018, the CPTPP positively impacts Vietnam, namely:

(a) The new agreement brings direct benefits to Vietnam, from trade liberalisation and improved market access. The elimination and reduction of around 18 000 tariff lines for Vietnam's export products under CPTPP provide reasons for multinational corporations to move into the country, especially in industries in which Vietnam enjoys comparative advantages, such as textiles and agriculture.
(b) CPTPP improves on Vietnam's current commitments to the WTO in a number of important sectors such as energy, mining, telecommunication and distribution.
(c) The CPTPP encourages the SOE reform process. Certain sectors that have traditionally been monopolised by SOEs, such as coal, electricity or petrol, are now opening to competition. The foreign ownership room in equitised SOEs has been expanded.
(d) The CPTPP also stimulates reforms in areas such as competition, services (including financial services, telecommunications, and temporary entry of service providers), customs, e-commerce, environment, government procurement, intellectual property, investment, labour standards, legal issues, market access for goods, rules of origin, non-tariff measures, and trade remedies.

[13] Another comprehensive trade agreement, the FTA between Vietnam and the EU (***EUVFTA***), was signed on 30 June 2019 and was ratified by the European Parliament on 12 February 2020, and by the National Assembly of Vietnam on 8 June 2020. The EUVFTA took effect on 1 August 2020. It provides expansive preferential treatment for both goods and services, recognition and protection of geographical indications for over 200 products, liberalised government procurement rules, and obligations relating to antitrust and mergers. It also contains sustainable development provisions, including legally binding rules on climate, labour, and human rights.

[14] Vietnam has been pursuing multilateral and bilateral FTAs with various partners. The following table summarises the recent ones:[11]

FTAs	*Status*
AFTA	Effective
ASEAN – China Free Trade Agreement	Effective
ASEAN – Korea Free Trade Agreement	Effective
ASEAN – Japan Comprehensive Economic Partnership	Effective
ASEAN – Australia – New Zealand Free Trade Agreement	Effective
ASEAN India Free Trade Agreement	Effective
Vietnam – Japan Economic Partnership Agreement	Effective
Vietnam – Chile Free Trade Agreement	Effective
Vietnam – Laos Trade Agreement	Signed on 3 March 2015
Vietnam – Korea Free Trade Agreement	Signed on 5 May 2015; effective from 20 December 2015
Vietnam – Eurasian Economic Union Free Trade Agreement	Signed on 29 May 2015; effective from October 2016
Vietnam – European Union Free Trade Agreement	Signed on 2 December 2015; effective from August 2020

[11] https://trungtamwto.vn/thong-ke/12065-tong-hop-cac-fta-cua-viet-nam-tinh-den-thang-112018; date of access: 20 Jul. 2023.

FTAs	*Status*
CPTPP	Signed on 8 March 2018; effective from November 2018
Regional Comprehensive Economic Partnership	Signed on 15 November 2020; effective from 1 Jan 2022
ASEAN – Hong Kong Free Trade Agreement	Signed on 12 November 2017; effective from 12 Feb 2021
Vietnam – United Kingdom Free Trade Agreement	Signed on 15 December 2020 and effective from 1 January 2021
Vietnam – Israel Free Trade Agreement	Signed on 25 July 2023
Ongoing negotiation: Vietnam – European Free Trade Association Free Trade Agreement	Negotiations commenced in May 2012
Ongoing negotiation: ASEAN – Canada	Re-starting negotiations in November 2021
Ongoing negotiation: Vietnam – UAE FTA	Negotiations are underway

1.3 Vietnam's Infrastructure: General

[15] Despite high levels of investment relative to GDP, the quality of Vietnam's infrastructure is still often rated by businesses and chambers of commerce in Vietnam as poor and a constraint on the growth of their businesses. Congested airports (until the advent of COVID-19) and busy roads are immediately apparent to any prospective foreign investor arriving in Hanoi or Ho Chi Minh City. Fortunately for Vietnam, investors in Asia have often seen worse.

[16] The state budget, official development assistance funds, and other public financial sources are limited. The Government is attempting to harness funds from the private sector and, in turn, has established a public-private partnership (***PPP***) regime to assist in this endeavour.[12] However, this has not proved successful. Although there is confusion in the press about what a PPP is, if one excludes build-operate-transfer (***BOT***) projects in the power sector (the basis for which pre-dates

[12] A new law on PPPs, Law No. 64/2020/QH14 on public-private partnership investment came into effect on 1 Jan. 2021 (the ***PPP Law***).

the PPP regulations), there have been no PPP projects under the PPP regulations which have been financed by private banks on a non-recourse basis.

[17] In the post-pandemic period, Vietnam views public infrastructure as an economic driver that can help overcome the pandemic's negative effects. As of 2022, Vietnam's infrastructure spending stands at 6% of its GDP, representing a significant increase from the 2.6% of GDP that was spent on infrastructure in 2016. For various reasons, the disbursement of public investment has been slower than expected. In recent months, there has been some improvement. However, many ministries, agencies, and provinces/ cities have been failing to meet the targets.[13]

1.4 Language

[18] Vietnamese is the official language. In written form, Vietnamese uses the Roman alphabet and accent marks to show sounds and tones. Few foreigners speak the language well.

[19] English is the most popular foreign language and is widely spoken, at least to a basic level, in urban areas. English study is common. For historical reasons, it is not uncommon to meet officials speaking fluent French, Russian, German, Czech and other East European languages, though the latter are becoming less common as the years elapse since it was more common to study in Poland and Bulgaria. In addition to European languages, more and more young Vietnamese are studying Chinese, Japanese and Korean in order to communicate with the investors from these countries.

1.5 Government and Political System

[20] The Socialist Republic of Vietnam is a single-party socialist republic. The President of Vietnam is the head of the State, and the Prime Minister of Vietnam is the head of Government, in a one-party system led by the Communist Party of Vietnam. The country is politically stable.[14]

[21] Assisting the Government in the management of the country are various line ministries. Each ministry is in charge of a specific sector. The ministries do not always see eye-to-eye on matters over which they have authority:

[13] Source: https://vietnamnews.vn/economy/1532862/disbursement-of-public-investment-capital-slows-in-4-months-of-2023.html.

[14] As a part of corruption campaigns, a number of some high-ranking officers (including central party members, ministers, military and police generals) have been disciplined in the last several years. Most recently, at the end of 2022, the President and two Deputy Prime Ministers resigned due to their 'political responsibilities' in corruption scandals during the COVID-19 pandemic. Observers take the view that the recent events should not affect the political system of Vietnam, nor do they change the viewpoints of the Government of Vietnam concerning foreign investment.

Ministries	*Sectors of Responsibility*
Government Inspectorate	Inspection, settlement of civil complaints and denunciations, anti-corruption.
Government Office	Assisting the Government in its management and operations.
Ministry of Agriculture and Rural Development	Agriculture, forestry, fisheries, rural development, animal breeds and medicine.
Ministry of Construction	Construction, architecture, development of urban areas and real estate.
Ministry of Culture, Sports and Tourism	Culture, sports, advertising, art and tourism.
Ministry of Education and Training	Education and training.
Ministry of Finance (***MOF***)	State budget, tax, State assets and loans, State capital used in State enterprises, securities market, customs, accounting and auditing.
Ministry of Foreign Affairs	Foreign affairs, international relations, consular affairs, management of Vietnamese people outside of Vietnam.
Ministry of Health	Health, medicine, drugs, cosmetics and food safety.
Ministry of Home Affairs	Management of State workforce, non-governmental organisations, State administrative reform.
Ministry of Industry and Trade (***MOIT***)	Industry, electricity, oil and gas, chemicals, food and drink, commerce, distribution, protection of consumer interests and competition.
Ministry of Information and Communications	Press, publishing, posts, telecommunications, internet, broadcasting and television, information technology and electronics.
Ministry of Justice	Development, implementation and review of laws.
Ministry of Labour, War Invalids and Social Affairs	Employment, salaries, social insurance, Vietnamese workers working overseas and foreigners working in Vietnam.

Ministries	*Sectors of Responsibility*
Ministry of National Defence	National defence.
Ministry of Natural Resources and Environment (***MONRE***)	Land, water and mineral resources, environment.
Ministry of Planning and-Investment (***MPI***)	Investment strategies, master plans and plans, development investment, domestic and foreign investment, Vietnam's overseas investment, overseas development assistance, enterprise establishment and management and statistics.
Ministry of Police	Public security, management of entrance/exit visas and residence of population.
Ministry of Science and Technology	Science and technology, intellectual property, standards, quality control, atomic energy and nuclear safety.
Ministry of Transport	Roads, railways, waterways, maritime, air and transport infrastructure.
State Bank of Vietnam (***SBV***)	Finance and banking, monetary and foreign exchange management.

1.6 Legal System

[22] Conceptually, Vietnam is a civil law country. Court judgments are not officially considered a source of law, judges do not have the power to interpret the law and court judgments are not binding in subsequent cases.[15]

[23] The Law on Promulgation of Legal Instruments[16] organises law into a hierarchy. The higher-ranking legal instruments set out general rules; the

[15] This will in theory change, at least in part. Under the Civil Code adopted in 2015, court precedents and equity principles (lẽ công bằng) can be used in respect of civil relations if there is no law or custom governing the same. Court precedents are those judgements that have been selected and announced by the Supreme People's Court for application by lower courts. So far, there have been sixty-three court precedents announced by Supreme People's Court (*see*, https://anle.toaan.gov.vn/webcenter/portal/anle/home; last access 26 Aug. 2023). Under the Civil Procedure Code adopted in 2015, 'equity principles' are those that are based on rightful principles accepted by society, and consistent with principles of humanity, impartiality and the equality of rights and obligations of parties to a dispute.

[16] Law on Promulgation of Legal Instruments No. 80/2015/QH13 of the National Assembly dated 22 Jun. 2015 (as amended by Law No. 63/2020/QH14 dated 18 Jun. 2020, effective from 1 Jan. 2021).

lower-ranking legal instruments provide an increasing level of detail. The hierarchy is as follows:

(a) The Constitution and laws are passed by the National Assembly and are the highest form of legal direction in Vietnam.
(b) Ordinances and resolutions are issued by the Standing Committee of the National Assembly when the National Assembly is not in session.
(c) Decrees are issued by the Government.
(d) Decisions are issued by the Prime Minister on the implementation of regulations.
(e) Circulars are issued by ministries and provide guidance on the implementation of decrees.

[24] Laws are enforced through the Vietnamese court system. This includes the Supreme People's Court, the People's High Courts in the North, Centre and South of Vietnam, the Provincial People's Courts in sixty-three cities and provinces, the District People's Courts and Military Courts.[17] For foreign investors, dispute resolution through the courts of Vietnam can sometimes be unpredictable and unsatisfactory.[18]

[25] The rulings of one court can generally be appealed to a higher authority.

[26] Under the Civil Procedure Code, all disputes, whether civil, commercial or labour, are subject to the same set of procedural rules. The recognition of foreign judgments and foreign arbitral awards falls under the jurisdiction of the relevant people's court.

1.7 Openness to Foreign Investment

[27] In theory, Vietnam treats foreign and domestic investors equally. In practice, however, certain nuances become evident, as demonstrated in the content of this work. With that said, such nuances do not detract from Vietnam's acclaimed openness to foreign investment, as highlighted by the World Bank's rankings for openness to trade (exports plus imports as a per cent of GDP), with Vietnam ranking in seventh place,[19] and further demonstrated by FDI amounting to about 4%–5% of GDP in recent years.[20]

[28] Vietnam's economy depends heavily on exports, with FDI companies being the main driver. For example, in 2022, FDI was responsible for around 74% of Vietnam's total exports.[21]

[17] Article 3 of the Law No. 62/2014/QH13 on Organisation of People's Courts of the National Assembly dated 24 Nov. 2014.

[18] *See* discussion in section 'Dispute Resolution: Vietnamese Courts' for further details.

[19] Data retrieved from https://www.theglobaleconomy.com/rankings/trade_openness/; date of access: 22 Jul. 2023.

[20] *Ibid.*

[21] Data retrieved from https://baodautu.vn/xuat-khau-phu-thuoc-fdi-cham-dap-ung-cac-tieu-chuan-thi-truong-d188342.html; date of access: 22 Jul. 2023.

[29] Many billions of dollars of FDI are registered every year, even during the COVID-19 pandemic. Statistics show that there was USD28.53 bn of newly added registered investment capital in 2020, a decline of 25% compared with the corresponding period of 2019.[22] It picked up again post-pandemic with the total foreign investment capital into Vietnam as of 31 December 2021 reaching USD38.9 bn, an increase of 25.2% compared to 2020. Given the recent turbulence of the global economy, 2022 saw a decrease of 24.6% compared to 2021, with total foreign investment capital into Vietnam of USD29.3 bn.[23]

[30] According to the MPI, Singapore has been the largest investor in Vietnam for three consecutive years. Japan, China, Korea, Hong Kong and Taiwan are other key investors in Vietnam.[24] Part of foreign investor confidence derives from the fact that the law recognises and protects an investor's ownership of assets, capital, revenue and other lawful rights and interests. More importantly, there have been few problems in practice, thus reassuring often anxious investors.

1.8 Current Trends

[31] Cross-border acquisitions have increased sharply in recent years, with various factors contributing to the rise:

(a) Vietnam's economy remains one of the most dynamic in Asia, with growth averaging 7% a year between 2000 and 2019. Vietnam's economy grew at about 3% in 2020 despite the coronavirus. Post-pandemic, Vietnam's economy experienced a strong rebound in 2022, with growth reaching 8%. Forecasts expect Vietnam's GDP growth to moderate level to 4.7% in 2023 and then to accelerate to 5.5% in 2024 and 6.0% in 2025.

(b) The Government of Vietnam continues to open markets to foreign investors:

  (i) A new Investment Law and a new Enterprise Law, which became effective on 1 January 2021, clarified the procedures applicable to acquisitions by foreigners of Vietnamese companies.

  (ii) By promulgating the list of 'market access conditions' in early 2021 (*see* section 'Acquisition of companies engaged in businesses that are subject to conditions'), the Government reduced uncertainty, making it easier for foreign investors to acquire an interest in Vietnamese companies.

  (iii) Since 2015, acquisitions by foreigners of the majority of a public company have become possible, provided the company takes the appropriate steps.

[22] Data retrieved from https://www.thestar.com.my/aseanplus/aseanplus-news/2020/12/31/foreign-investors-pump-over-us285bil-into-vietnam-in-2020.

[23] Data retrieved from https://www.mpi.gov.vn/portal/Pages/2023-6-28/Tinh-hinh-thu-hut-dau-tu-nuoc-ngoai-6-thang-dau-nafv0c86.aspx; date of access: 22 Jul. 2023.

[24] Data retrieved from https://www.mpi.gov.vn/portal/Pages/2023-6-28/Tinh-hinh-thu-hut-dau-tu-nuoc-ngoai-6-thang-dau-nafv0c86.aspx; date of access: 22 Jul. 2023.

(iv) New FTAs (including high-quality FTAs such as CPTPP and EUVFTA) coming into effect unlock opportunities for both Vietnamese companies to access global markets and foreign investors to invest in Vietnam.

(c) Not only is Vietnam politically stable, but the country has also managed to maintain its economic stability. Due to increasing foreign exchange reserves, Vietnam can retain a relatively stable Vietnamese Dong/US Dollar exchange rate, as demonstrated during the challenging period of 2022 and 2023, when the Vietnamese Dong appreciated slightly against the US Dollar.

(d) Despite Government efforts to reduce interest rates, Vietnamese Dong interest rates for loans remain between 6% and 10% for the average business, and loans are not always obtainable as a result of issues within the banking system. Consequently, many businesses have been financed through equity contributions, more specifically by investors who are subsequently willing to cash out.

(e) In some sectors, it can be difficult for new entrants to break into the market except through acquisitions:

(i) Vietnam has a policy of disallowing the establishment of new market players in certain sectors, such as finance companies and securities companies. In this instance, in order to access the Vietnamese market, the acquisition of existing companies is the only option for foreign investors.

(ii) In the brewery sector, a limited number of companies dominate the distribution networks; thus, starting a new beer business of any size is costly and difficult.[25]

(iii) Healthcare is a further example: it is difficult and takes considerable time for a new investor to find land and develop a new hospital; hence, an acquisition of an existing hospital is the quickest way for the investor to expand their business in Vietnam.[26]

(f) Vietnam is considered by multinational companies as a promising destination for the 'China plus one' policy, given its relatively cheap labour cost, particularly in sectors such as electronics manufacturing and supply chain industries. However, it may take time to develop greenfield projects of this nature, so acquisitions are sometimes a more realistic option. This trend accelerated when the relationship between the US and China became tense.

(g) While Vietnam's focused funds, such as VinaCapital, Mekong Capital and Dragon Capital, are still active in Vietnam, after more than twenty years of development, many Vietnamese companies have now developed to a size that is attractive to the larger international funds. For example:

[25] At the end of 2017, Thai Beverage bought a 54% stake in the main brewer in the south of Vietnam. In January 2016, TCC Group, the largest investor in Berli Jucker PCL (BJC), purchased Metro Cash & Carry Vietnam from German Metro Group. Also in 2016, Central Group and Nguyen Kim Group jointly acquired Big C Vietnam for EUR920 m (USD1.05 bn).

[26] In 2013, Clermont acquired 80% interests in Hoan My hospital group from Fortis Healthcare and then increased to 100% in 2015. More recently, in 2022, CVC purchased 60% of Phuong Chau hospitals, chain of maternal and infant hospital in southern of Vietnam. Thomson Medical just announced the signing of contract to buy 100% of FV Hospital. There are a number of transactions are also on going at the time of writing this article.

(i) KKR first invested in Masan Consumer in 2011, when it purchased a 10% stake for USD159 m in what was, at the time, the largest private equity deal in Vietnam. In 2013, it increased its stake in Masan Consumer to USD359 m. In July 2015, KKR was reported to have sold half of its holding to an undisclosed buyer for a 100% return. In 2020, it led a consortium that acquired a minority stake in the Vietnamese real estate developer Vinhomes for USD650 m. KKR was not the first to invest in Masan Consumer. VinaCapital and Mekong Capital had done so well before KKR and also made good returns.

(ii) In 2013, Warburg Pincus, leading a consortium that included Credit Suisse, acquired an interest in the retail assets of Vingroup, one of the largest private-sector property developers. This was the largest initial private equity investment in Vietnam at that time and was followed by an additional follow-on round.

(iii) After the success of its investment in Masan Group in 2013, TPG also made other investments in Vietnam, including the investment in Vietnam Australia International School which was acquired from Mekong Capital and MajInvest in 2017.

(iv) The pace of investments and acquisitions has accelerated in recent years, with the exception of the interruption due to the COVID-19 pandemic. KKR made further investments of USD250 m in several companies of Masan Group in 2017, led a consortium, including Credit Suisse and Temasek, investing USD650 m in Vinhomes in 2020, and made another investment of USD100 m into Equest in 2021.

(v) In 2019, Temasek invested in Ho Chi Minh City-headquartered Scommerce Investment Corporation. Scommerce is the parent company of delivery start-ups GHN and AhaMove. GHN and AhaMove have been delivery partners for Vietnam's four largest e-commerce platforms – Shopee, Tiki, Sendo, and Lazada – as well as over 100 000 online small and medium-sized merchants.

(vi) At the end of 2020, GIC closed a USD200 m minority investment in Vinmec International General Hospital JSC (***Vinmec***), a subsidiary of local conglomerate Vingroup and the owner and operator of seven hospitals in Vietnam, as well as a number of clinics and pharmacies across the country.

(vii) From 2018–2021, SK Group invested USD410 m in buying 16.26% of WinCommerce, USD345 m to buy a 4.9% stake in The CrownX of Masan Group, and nearly USD1 bn to purchase a 6.1% stake in Vingroup. SK also acquired interests in several other companies, including pharmaceutical retail chain Pharmacity and pharmaceutical company Imexpharm Corp.

(viii) In June 2021, a group of investors, including Alibaba Group and Baring Private Equity Asia (BPEA), invested USD400 m to acquire a 5.5% stake in The CrownX.

(ix) Warburg Pincus has been investing in Asia real estate companies and platforms for over fifteen years and is one of the largest and most active investors in Asian real estate today, with over USD7.0 bn invested and over USD1.5 bn committed in Vietnam since 2013, in addition to completing two of the largest IPOs ever in the country, Vincom Retail and Techcombank.

(x) In July 2021, VNLife raised USD250 m in its Series B round. VNLife has been financially backed by eight investors, including Dragoneer Investment Group and General Atlantic.

(xi) In September 2022, CVC invested in Phuong Chau Trade and Investment JSC, the operator of the Phuong Chau-branded hospitals.

(h) A constant challenge facing private equity firms is that the investment opportunities in Vietnam tend to be smaller than their funds are targeting. This can sometimes force funds to be creative. Although this issue also reduces the number of deals, the smaller private equity funds are now creating deals for the larger funds as follows:

(i) The Standard Chartered Private Equity investments provided successful exits for earlier-stage private equity investors. Its Golden Gate investment allowed a fund managed by Mekong Capital, a Vietnamese private equity firm, to make a full exit with a reported net multiple of 9x, while the USD90 m purchase of Loc Troi Group stake from VinaCapital's Vietnam Opportunity Fund and DWS was one of the larger Vietnam PE exits via a secondary sale.

(ii) Mekong was again the beneficiary of the trend when it sold its interest in the Vietnam Australia School to TPG.

(iii) In 2019, Abraaj exited Vietnam-USA Society English Centres (VUS), while Baring Private Equity Asia acquired the English teaching centres.

(iv) In March 2022, CDH Investments and Partners Group sold a significant minority stake of around 36% in Golden Gate to Temasek and some other investors.

1.9 Sector Trends

(a) Banks and Finance Companies

[32] The most vibrant acquisitive behaviour over the last fifteen years has been in the financial sector, with the first wave of investments around fifteen years ago. ANZ Bank (Australia), Banque Nationale de Paris (France), Commonwealth Bank (Australia), Deutsche Bank (Germany), HSBC (UK), Societe Generale (France), Standard Chartered (UK), United Overseas Bank (Singapore), OCBC (Singapore), Maybank (Malaysia), International Finance Corporation and various others have bought (and often sold, not necessarily at a worthwhile – or indeed any – profit) strategic interests in local Vietnamese banks, despite all the regulatory hurdles.

[33] Following the first wave of somewhat unsuccessful investments by Western banks, Japanese and Korean banks have become key investors in the financial sector in Vietnam. The following examples highlight this:

(i) In 2011, Mizuho Corporate Bank Ltd. purchased 15% of the Joint Stock Commercial Bank for Foreign Trade of Vietnam (***Vietcombank***). Shortly after, in 2012, Bank of Tokyo Mitsubishi UFJ purchased a 20% strategic stake in Vietnam Joint Stock Commercial Bank of Industry and Trade (***Vietinbank***), another State-owned commercial bank. These were the biggest acquisitions in Vietnam's financial sector at the time.

(ii) In 2019, KEB Hana Bank acquired 15% of the Bank for Investment and Development of Vietnam (BIDV) and became the first foreign strategic shareholder of the bank.

(iii) Even more recently, Sumitomo Mitsui Banking Corporation agreed to acquire a 15% stake in Vietnam Prosperity Joint Stock Commercial Bank (VPBank) at another record consideration.

[34] Aside from strategic investors, banks also draw interest from financial investors. For example, Warburg Pincus bought into Techcombank after HSBC had withdrawn.

[35] Alongside this influx of Asian banks following the exit of Western banks in Vietnam, Shinhan Vietnam Bank bought ANZ's retail business in Vietnam. Furthermore, in March 2023, UOB completed the purchase of Vietnam's consumer banking business from Citibank.

[36] Further bank acquisitions are expected in the near future, with various banks planning to raise capital. Many banks plan to increase their charter capital in 2023 and 2024 in order to ensure operational safety in addition to having more resources for business development. For example, in June 2023, the SBV allowed Vietcombank to increase its registered capital by 18% to USD2.4 bn. Vietinbank is also expected to raise its registered capital by 37.3% to USD2.6 bn.

[37] In addition to bank acquisitions, non-bank financial institutions have attracted acquirers. Because of the SBV's policy not to grant licences for new finance companies, foreign investors have little option but to buy interests in existing companies. The most notable transaction was the investment of USD1.37 bn by SMBC to VPBank's subsidiary, FE Credit, for a 49% stake. More recently, the Saigon Hanoi Commercial Joint Stock Bank (SHB) transferred 100% of the capital at SHB Finance to MUFG's Krungsri. Earlier, Credit Saison had acquired an interest in HD SAISON; in 2018, Prudential sold 100% of its consumer finance business in Vietnam, Prudential Vietnam Finance Company Limited to Shinhan Card Co., Ltd.

(b) Real Estate

[38] For a populous country like Vietnam, good land is rare and increasingly precious.

[39] The real estate sector was booming in the late 2010s. For example, in 2019, South Korea's SK Group invested about USD1 bn in Vingroup. In 2020, KKR acquired a minority stake in Vietnamese real estate developer Vinhomes for USD650 m. This followed a trend, started by Warburg Pincus, which first bought into the retail assets of Vingroup in 2013. GIC, one of the investment arms of the Government of Singapore, also has a stake in Vinhomes, which it acquired for about USD1 bn.

[40] After the boom in the late 2010s, the real estate market softened. When the Government tightened the bond market, the main channel of capital raising for real estate developers, many real estate developers suffered from a shortage of liquidity.

[41] The focus has now shifted to industrial land in anticipation of the expected surge in factories moving out of China and warehouses for logistics operations. Provincial markets with large-scale industrial parks, such as Bac Ninh, Bac Giang, Thai Nguyen, Hai Phong, and Hai Duong, will still develop due to the demand for real estate in the vicinity of the industrial zone. This shift towards industrial land is also demonstrated by the established venture between Warburgs and Becamex, with large foreign companies such as LOGOS now also investing. Further examples include:

(i) At the beginning of January 2022, GLP established GLP Vietnam Development Partners I with a total investment of USD1.1 bn in six logistics centre projects with a total area of up to 900 000 m^2.
(ii) In February 2022, BW Industrial Development Joint Stock Company, an industrial real estate developer co-founded by Warburg Pincus and Becamex IDC, announced the acquisition of roughly 74 000 m^2 of land in Bac Tien Phong Industrial Park in Quang Ninh province, developed by DEEP C.
(iii) CapitaLand Development announced the signing of a memorandum of understanding on investment cooperation with the People's Committee of Bac Giang province. The two sides will promote the development of an urban-industrial-logistics project with a total area of more than 400 hectares across the province, with an investment commitment of USD1 bn.

(c) Energy

[42] Foreign companies were historically active as buyers and sellers of energy businesses, particularly power, oil and gas. Not all of this is driven by local factors. BP's sale of its Nam Con Son gas-to-power project was driven by its desire to sell assets around the world after the Gulf of Mexico disaster. ConocoPhillips also sold its Vietnam assets to realign its global priorities. Chevron sold its interest in the South-West gas-to-power project (offshore Blocks B and 52 to the still putative O Mon/Kien Giang power complexes).

[43] Just before the Ukraine-Russia war began, in May 2021, Russian state-owned oil and gas producer Zarubezhneft agreed to buy out compatriot Rosneft's shareholdings in two offshore exploration and development projects in Vietnam, along with a related offshore gas and condensate pipeline. Later, in August 2021, Bitexco Energy Ltd signed a share purchase agreement with Repsol Exploración SA to acquire 100% of Repsol's shares in Talisman (Vietnam 15-2/01) Ltd.

[44] Much of the current activity is in the acquisition of renewable energy projects, particularly by companies from Thailand, such as B. Grimm Power, Super Energy and Gunkul Engineering. Often, this is driven by the difficulty faced by foreign companies in developing a project themselves, so local developers sell to foreign interests when key milestones have been achieved; these foreign interests sometimes on-sell to foreign utilities seeking to burnish their less-than-green credentials.

[45] M&A activities in the renewable energy industry still have great potential, especially after the adoption of the National Power Development Plan for the period of 2021–2030, with a vision to 2050 (PDP8) in May 2023. Under PDP8, coal power, which currently accounts for 34% of electricity generation in Vietnam, will peak by 2030, and be reduced to zero by 2050. Renewables will increase their share of electricity generation from 25% in 2020 to a baseline of 31% in 2030 and 68% in 2050. Some recent transactions in this space include: EDP Renewables acquired 87% of Sunseap; ACEN bought 49% of Sola NT Holding; B.Grimm Power acquired 80% of TTVN's 48MW Quang Tri wind power project. In addition, B.Grimm Power acquired the 240MWp Tay Ninh Solar Power Plant; Sustainable Hitachi acquired a 35% stake in Trung Nam's 152MW wind farm. JERA, through its subsidiary JERA Asia, acquired an interest in Gia Lai Electricity Joint Stock Company from International Finance Corporation and Armstrong.

(d) Education, Healthcare and Pharmaceuticals

[46] Education, healthcare and pharmaceuticals are currently popular sectors in Vietnam. KKR, TPG, EQT, the Partner Group, Baring, Navis and Inspired are just some of the private equity houses whose desire to do good and to do well are converging in one or more of these areas. Another sub-sector, EdTech (which combines Education and Technology), is still in its early stages but has attracted the attention of investors.

[47] The improvement in living conditions and growing income (and some would say poorer eating habits) have resulted in higher spending on healthcare services. However, the quality of these services has a varied reputation and a visit to the hospital was generally not recommended except in extreme cases. However, GIC's investment in Vinmec, VinaCapital's Vietnam Opportunity Fund's investment in Thu Cuc International General Hospital, a private healthcare company in Hanoi, and CVC's investment in Vietnam-based Phuong Chau-branded hospitals will attempt to reverse these negative perceptions of the healthcare sector.

[48] The increasing interest from foreign investors in the pharmaceuticals sector is partially due to the market becoming more open. Pharmaceuticals have witnessed several M&A transactions, including between Mekophar (Vietnam) and Nipro Pharma (Japan), Imexpharm (Vietnam) and SK Group (Korea), Pymepharco (Vietnam) and STADA Service Holdings BV (Germany), and Hataphar (Vietnam) and ASKA Pharmaceutical (Japan).

(e) Consumer and Retail

[49] As a country with a growing middle class, the consumer sector is becoming increasingly attractive. Jardine Cycle & Carriage paid almost USD1 bn for about 10% of Vinamilk. Swire Coca-Cola Ltd., a wholly-owned subsidiary of Swire Pacific Ltd., announced in January 2023 the completion of its acquisition of Coca-Cola Beverages Vietnam Ltd., the Coca-Cola bottling subsidiary in Vietnam. Furthermore, funds managed by Mekong Capital have regularly bought smaller consumer-oriented companies.

[50] In February 2023, Thailand's Central Retail Corporation announced that it will double the number of its Vietnam stores, with its largest-ever local investment of USD1.45 bn. The chain will jump to over six hundred stores in fifty-seven of sixty-three cities and provinces over the next five years. The Thai company also plans to renovate ten to twelve Nguyen Kim chain electronics supermarkets while opening an additional three to five new supermarkets and Go! Hypermarkets. Similarly, Japan's Aeon plans to operate one hundred supermarkets across Vietnam by 2025. Likewise, South Korean retail giant Lotte has also said it will open more supermarkets in Vietnam. After gradually withdrawing from China, Lotte now regards Vietnam as its third most important market after South Korea and Japan.

(f) E-commerce and Logistics

[51] E-commerce and logistics are also active. With 70% of the population under thirty-five years of age and a frighteningly high smartphone penetration, rapid growth is inevitable in these sectors.

(i) E-commerce

[52] The COVID-19 pandemic spurred the growth of the online ecosystem, led by the e-commerce industry. With the explosion of online businesses, Vietnam's logistics and warehousing industry has many development opportunities.

[53] In the last ten years, there were two major phases in the development of the e-commerce sector. Until around 2017, market players were mainly domestic e-commerce platforms, and their presence was relatively modest. After 2017, a number of global companies such as Alibaba, JD.com, Amazon, Shinhan Bank and Mizuho have all invested in the Vietnamese e-commerce market through services such as Shopee, Lazada, Tiki and Momo. During these years, Gross Merchandise Value increased from USD1.5 bn to an estimated USD14 bn in 2021. E-commerce retail sales climbed from 1.2% to 7%, and the annual average growth rate skyrocketed to 56%.

(ii) Logistics

[54] In 2019, Scommerce, the parent company of start-ups GiaoHangNhanh (GHN) and AhaMove, wrapped up a funding round led by Temasek which was worth up to USD100 m. Another last-mile delivery company, Giao Hang Tiet Kiem (GHTK), is aiming for a domestic IPO at a USD1 bn valuation to raise capital and combat the increasing competition in the logistics sector.

[55] VinaCapital and Mekong Capital have been acquiring interests in various logistics and platform companies.

(g) Food & Beverage

[56] After the COVID-19 pandemic, the food and beverage sector recovered quickly. In March 2022, CDH and the Partner Group sold 32.9% of Golden Gate to a group of buyers led by Temasek. In December 2022, Jollibee was reportedly in negotiations to sell 10%–15% of its shares in Highlands Coffee, a coffee and fast-food chain, to an investor valued at USD800 m. In July 2023, Vietnamese conglomerate NovaGroup sold its F&B business to a Singaporean firm.

(h) Technology, Telecom and Media

[57] Chinese giants Alibaba and Tencent have historically been openly acquisitive (although the Vietnamese show some quiet concern); Grab acquired Uber's South-East Asia operations, including Vietnam; however, this seems to have opened up room for competition, thus resulting in almost immediate success for the pleasing green of the Go-Jek motorbike helmet.

[58] With a young, dynamic population of around 100 m, the number of internet users in Vietnam is increasing rapidly. More than 70% of Vietnam's population has access to the internet, of whom nearly 50% have shopped online, 53% of them using e-wallets.

[59] From the beginning of 2021, Vietnam's biggest e-wallet company, MoMo, has raised at least USD100 m from six global investors, including Warburg Pincus, as part of plans to become a 'super-app' and go public by 2025. Fintech gained more traction during the COVID-19 pandemic, with retail moving online and consumers looking for more contactless payment options. In July 2021, VNLIFE, a leading technology company pioneering the development of Vietnam's digital ecosystem, announced that it had raised over USD250 m in a Series B funding round led by General Atlantic and Dragoneer Investment Group, with participation from PayPal Ventures and EDBI. Existing investors GIC and SoftBank Vision Fund 1 also participated in the round.

[60] In February 2023, Masan invested USD105 m in Trust IQ to develop artificial intelligence applications in retail and consumer finance for its customers. Masan has also cooperated with Techcombank to create the WINLife ecosystem to draw on the personal financial needs of customers who are using Masan's retail and consumer services.

1.10 Sourcing Deals and Obstacles to Deals

[61] As of December 2021, there were around 857 551 licensed active companies in Vietnam.[27] In 2022 and the first six months of 2023, 321 918 new companies were established, and 243 224 companies ceased operation either temporarily or permanently.[28] Currently, there are nearly 1 m operating companies, though many of these are so small as to probably be invisible even to the trained tax man.

[62] As of 30 December 2022, the SSC reported via its official website that 743 companies were listed on the Ho Chi Minh Stock Exchange (***HOSE***) and the Hanoi

[27] Data retrieved from https://www.gso.gov.vn/wp-content/uploads/2022/11/Sach-trang-DN-2022.pdf.

[28] Data retrieved from https://dangkykinhdoanh.gov.vn/vn/tin-tuc/597/6407/tinh-hinh-dang-ky-doanh-nghiep-thang-12-va-nam-2022.aspx and https://dangkykinhdoanh.gov.vn/vn/tin-tuc/598/6544/tinh-hinh-dang-ky-doanh-nghiep-thang-6-va-6-thang-dau-nam-2023.aspx.

Stock Exchange (***HNX***),[29] and 856 companies were registered for trading on the Unlisted Public Companies (***UPCom***) market.[30]

[63] The large number of privately-owned businesses in Vietnam should, in theory, offer a wide range of options for foreign buyers. However, publicly available financial information and other data on the vast majority of Vietnamese companies remains limited.

[64] Most buyers use existing relationships or their knowledge of the market to source transactions. Intermediaries are sometimes used as a source of identifying targets, but few have a broad reach.

[65] Most buyers will spend substantial time and consider a large number of opportunities before investing. Concerns about deal quality and the small size of most targets are major barriers to finding suitable targets.

[66] Common obstacles to concluding deals include the following:

(a) Many targets have a number of skeletons in the cupboard. One example is a target having two (or more) sets of accounts and consequent tax issues. Another example is a target that engages in behaviour that would amount to a breach of anti-bribery and corruption laws. In some cases, sellers may be unable to dispose of the skeletons. In other cases, they do not know how to work their way out of the problem before commencing a transaction. If they fail to disclose the problem upfront, which is not uncommon, the seller's loss of credibility damages the prospects for the remainder of the transaction.
(b) For various historical, cultural and legal reasons, Vietnamese businessmen are used to changing the terms of a deal as it moves forward, including terms concerning price or deal structure. This can occur even after contracts have been signed. They sometimes do not understand that the foreign view of the rhythm of a negotiation presupposes that a deal term, once agreed upon, tends not to be changed unless some other fundamental tenet of the deal has changed.
(c) Targets trying to achieve high prices often provide overly optimistic forecasts of their performance at the start of a transaction. If this is followed by failure to come close to such forecasts during the inevitably protracted timelines involved in an acquisition of a Vietnamese company, the transaction can come apart. Unsophisticated sellers sometimes misunderstand valuation and pricing concepts, such as enterprise value versus equity value and fixed or locked-box versus completion accounts price, so they are disappointed and decide to walk away from the transaction when they realise the actual consideration.
(d) Vietnamese companies often lack adequate professional assistance. This is sometimes linked to the issue of the skeletons in the cupboard, with the

[29] Data retrieved from https://www.ssc.gov.vn/cs/idcplg?IdcService=GET_FILE&dID=125214&dDocName=APPSSCGOVVN1620125375&allowInterrupt=1 (accessed on 25 Jul. 2023).
[30] *Ibid.*

owner unable to open up to advisers. However, this problem is slowly reducing in importance as Vietnamese companies are taking a more structured approach for medium and large domestic deals or cross-border deals. These deals now tend to involve advisors at a minimum, as shareholders see the benefits of having an official process and professional advice in terms of a better equity valuation and terms and an increase in the likelihood of the deal completing.

(e) In many instances, target companies are used to doing a variety of unrelated businesses. There is sometimes no clear separation between personal assets and company assets, or one group company is used for raising capital for another group company's business. Without having a proper set-up, coupled with administrative and licensing challenges (e.g., in some locations, because of their own internal issues, the licensing authorities simply freeze any applications for land transfer), it is sometimes impossible (or takes too much time) to restructure the group to sell the target business or close the transaction.

(f) Many companies are still owned or controlled by their founders. Obstacles sometimes arise from the fact that such founders place too much focus on issues that are relatively insignificant due to the emotional toil involved in selling a company that they have built. Likewise, officials of State-owned companies that are up for sale, who might have their own personal concerns, may be reluctant to provide sufficient cooperation to enable the buyer to undertake proper due diligence or conclude the deal.

1.11 Vietnam: Risks

[67] More and more investors have been investigating possible investments in Vietnam. Investment in Vietnam entails certain risks that need to be managed. Below are some of the risks that foreign investors tend to consider and attempt to mitigate where necessary.

(a) Predictability

[68] Vietnamese laws contain many gaps, contradictions and internal inconsistencies, and many Vietnamese counterparties are not used to detailed international standard contracts. While the laws and contract standards are constantly improving, there is still a heightened risk of misunderstanding and disputes as a result of the vagueness of the law and normal contract standards. If a dispute cannot be solved informally, as usually occurs in practice, there is an appreciable risk of an unsatisfactory outcome for a foreign investor. Given the absence of a meaningful system of binding case laws or other interpretative aids of binding precedential value,[31] as well as the lack of experienced judges and arbitrators, the results of court and arbitral proceedings tend to be more unpredictable than in many other jurisdictions.

[31] As observed in footnote 18, this may change over the course of time.

[69] The best means of mitigating these risks is for foreign investors to spend substantial time and resources building a relationship with their contractual counterparties. In addition, but possibly as a secondary matter, for many projects, it may be possible for the choice of a foreign law and a foreign dispute resolution forum to limit the risk of legal disputes.

(b) Enforcement Risks

[70] It can be difficult to enforce a contractual term in Vietnam, especially against a powerful Vietnamese company that has strong connections with and strong influence on government entities, businesses and other stakeholders in Vietnam.

[71] While an investor may manage to get Vietnamese counterparties to agree on a foreign court or foreign arbitration as a dispute resolution body, the judgment or decision of a foreign court from most developed jurisdictions will not be recognised in Vietnam. The award or decision of a foreign arbitration cannot be directly enforced but has to go through the court's recognition process.

[72] In many instances, an investor has to accept a Vietnamese court or arbitration as a dispute resolution body. The courts in Vietnam are generally not independent from the Government, and observers frequently question how free they are from inappropriate influences. Although Vietnamese arbitration is generally considered to be more neutral than the Vietnamese courts, there is no guarantee that all the arbitrators hearing the case will be free from inappropriate influences.

[73] Even if an investor did prevail in court or arbitration, it would have to rely on the provincial judgment enforcement body to enforce the award. So, even if the investor wins the case, there is no guarantee that it will be able to enforce the award.

[74] The result of the time taken by litigation/arbitration, the cost of the proceedings and the lack of certainty about any result means that few disputes of size are brought to court or arbitration in Vietnam. Those that are brought to court or arbitration in Vietnam tend to be terminated or settled before a decision.

[75] As legal action is a last resort of dubious value, it is more important to ensure that the interests of all parties are aligned, such that Vietnamese counterparties are incentivised to comply with contractual terms.

(c) Foreign Ownership Restrictions

[76] Foreign ownership in certain sectors is restricted (or prohibited) under international treaties (such as the WTO commitments or FTAs) or domestic law (*see* section 'Foreign ownership limits'). If international treaties and domestic laws are silent, the licensing authority has the discretion to decide whether or not to allow foreign investment into the relevant sector.

[77] In some sectors, foreign investors (because of written or unwritten regulations) are required to cooperate with a Vietnamese party to set up joint ventures. It is often difficult for foreign investors to investigate which Vietnamese partner would be most appropriate. This is because of a lack of reliable public information about businesses and individuals. Private investigations are possible, but they are rarely effective, at least without the knowledge and consent of the person being

investigated. Once a Vietnamese partner has been chosen, it is necessary to maintain a good relationship with such a partner during the course of operations of the joint venture. This requires a solid meeting of the minds at the beginning on the purpose and goals of the company. The corporate documents should also be well drafted to reflect such intentions. They should also embed realistic management rights in favour of both investors in the company. This includes, most importantly, agreed rights in respect of the appointment of the general director, who is normally the legal representative of the company and hence has substantial day-to-day power over the affairs of the company.

(d) Development Risk

[78] In some sectors, it is straightforward for investors to obtain the necessary licences and permits, including an investment registration certificate (or an amendment to an existing investment registration certificate in the case of an investment made by way of acquisition). But for large projects or those in sensitive areas, developments can take a long time. This is because large numbers of governmental bodies are involved in the licensing process and because the administrative system is neither transparent nor efficient. It is useful to understand the licensing parameters upfront as well as to get to know those responsible for implementing them.

(e) Licensing Issues

[79] Vietnam is a bureaucratic country. Numerous licences, permits and approvals are required by every business. The fact that investors receive an investment registration certificate does not mean that their project can be built or be operated until all other permits, approvals and consents relevant to the construction or operation have been obtained. This results in delays and additional costs to businesses. The impact of the various licensing requirements is often small if the regulations are followed. But, there is a cost of obtaining and monitoring the necessary licences. Businesses should have a detailed list of the required licences and permits so that, at least during the development phase, there are no surprises.

(f) Land Use Rights

[80] Good land in Vietnam is limited, and there are often many people competing for it. Land that is suitable for any given investment project may therefore sometimes be difficult to find. It can also be more expensive than investors initially expect.

[81] New foreign investors should ensure that they receive their land use right certificate in the name of their newly established company with the appropriate land use purpose before making any substantial capital contributions to their projects. If they lease land, they should conduct a thorough check on the status of the land, as well as the right of the lessor to enter into the lease. This should reduce risks, including the risk of invalidity and unexpected land plans that may cause the land to be taken back in the future or the risk that the company is required to make any additional payments to the State or other parties.

[82] If foreign investors acquire an interest in an existing company that owns or leases buildings, they should conduct a thorough investigation into the status of the building, including licences or permits allowing the developer to build the property and for the existing target company to use and occupy the property for the business that it is currently doing or planning to do.

(g) Employment Law

[83] Vietnamese employment law is generally protective of the employee. In addition, employment tribunals tend to resolve disputes in favour of the employee. The adoption of carefully drafted internal labour rules is an important legal factor in ensuring labour harmony and protecting an employer's rights. If a dispute arises, employers should (if possible and appropriate in the circumstances) find an approach that avoids unnecessary legal processes.

(h) Foreign Exchange

[84] The Vietnamese Dong is not a freely convertible currency and may not be taken out of Vietnam easily. Foreign-owned projects which receive revenue in Vietnamese Dong will be exposed to: (i) devaluations in the value of the Vietnamese Dong until such revenues can be converted into foreign currency; (ii) the risk that there is no foreign currency available at the time of conversion; and (iii) the fact that currency cannot be converted or remitted except at specific times (e.g., once a year in respect of dividends).

[85] A Vietnamese company can only convert funds into foreign currency and remit overseas for limited purposes. Dividends and capital gains can be freely remitted but only after the financial year's end or the completion of a sales transaction. It is often possible to use shareholder loans and other agreements to achieve greater flexibility with respect to the timing of foreign exchange payments.

[86] Investment and divestment activities of a foreign investor may have to be done via specific bank accounts in Vietnam. This sometimes creates significant hurdles for executing cross-border transactions.

(i) Tax

[87] Tax rates differ depending on the nature of the seller entity and the target entity. For instance, a foreign institutional seller is subject to a capital gain tax of 20% of the gains if it sells shares in a non-public company and 0.1% of the transaction value if it sells shares in a public company; and a foreign institutional seller is not required to pay profit remittance tax. A Vietnamese individual seller is only required to pay 0.1% of the transaction value whether the target company is a public or non-public JSC, but they must pay a 5% personal income tax on dividends distributed to him. A Vietnamese institutional seller is required to pay 20% of the gains whether the target company is a public or non-public JSC. Because of the different treatments, it can be difficult to structure a transaction that optimises tax results for all sellers.

[88] The lack of guidance on the declaration and payment of indirect capital gains tax in case of an offshore transaction limits the ability of the parties to agree on different deal structures to achieve their goals. Furthermore

[89] Certain tax rights can be difficult to enforce, such as those arising out of tax treaties.

[90] The tax authorities are currently agitated about perceived transfer pricing abuses by multinational companies. The tax authorities have limited properly trained manpower, which means that active enforcement of tax laws is unpredictable and can be viewed as arbitrary.

[91] There are also significant issues for foreign-invested companies regarding tax audits conducted using new interpretations of the regulations that are enforced retroactively. Penalties and interest can add significantly to the tax invoice as a result of audits that occur many years after the fact.

(j) Import and Distribution

[92] While foreign companies can obtain import and distribution licences in many sectors, these are often limited in practice. A foreign-invested company engaged in distribution must apply for a business licence. In addition, a foreign-invested company engaged in retailing must apply for a licence to open each new outlet after the first one and (with some limited exceptions such as small shops in retail malls) the opening of such outlet is conditional upon the satisfaction of an economic need test (ENT). Difficulties in opening more than one retail outlet and the ENT should be removed for investors from CPTPP Member States in January 2024 (five years following the entry into force of CPTPP concerning Vietnam).

(k) Corruption

[93] Vietnam has strict anti-bribery laws which, despite general appearances to the contrary, are sometimes enforced. For both foreign and domestic compliance reasons, employees should be appropriately trained in how to do business without bribery. Businesses that do not engage in corrupt acts are widely respected. Many foreign companies do not engage in corrupt acts and manage to do good business. Indeed, there is sometimes an impression that a strict line on the subject of corruption makes business easier as officials will concentrate their time on other 'more productive' businesses. But clearly, this can be easier or harder depending on the sector involved and the level of demand for each company's products or services.

2 CORPORATE FRAMEWORK

2.1 Business Vehicles

[94] There are various types of incorporated and unincorporated entities in Vietnam. The viability and structure of an acquisition depend substantially on the type of entity being purchased. The main entities in existence are:

(a) Joint stock companies (***JSCs***), limited liability companies (***LLCs***) with one member, LLCs with two or more members, partnerships and private enterprises, all of which are subject to the Enterprise Law.[32]
(b) Public companies, i.e., JSCs which have 100 or more non-major shareholders (excluding professional securities investors) holding at least 10% of the voting shares and a charter capital of at least VND30 bn (approximately USD1 276 596) or more.[33] JSCs are still treated as public companies even if they do not meet the condition in the preceding sentence if such JSCs had been listed on the HOSE or HNX or registered for trading on the UPCom before 1 January 2021.[34] Public companies are subject to both the Enterprise Law and the Securities Law.
(c) Joint venture companies and wholly foreign-owned companies which were originally established under the former law on foreign investment in Vietnam and which have not re-registered to become companies governed by the Enterprise Law. These are slowly becoming extinct.
(d) SOEs[35] which can only be purchased in accordance with the regulations on State capital divestment or equitisation.[36]
(e) Cooperatives, which are subject to the Law on Cooperatives.[37] We do not examine this type of entity further in this chapter.
(f) Business cooperation contracts between two or more parties to conduct joint business operations in Vietnam and to share the revenues or the profits in an agreed manner.[38] These are effectively unincorporated joint ventures. As such, they fall outside the purview of this work.

2.2 Effect of Corporate Form on Acquisitions

[95] Most transactions in Vietnam involve the acquisitions of JSCs and LLCs. Although these two types of companies share a number of characteristics, such as limiting the liability of company owners to the amount of their capital

[32] Law on Enterprises No. 59/2020/QH14 of the National Assembly dated 17 Jun. 2020 which came into force on 1 Jan. 2021 (***Enterprise Law***).

[33] Article 32 of Law on Securities No. 54/2019/QH14 of the National Assembly dated 26 Nov. 2019, which came into force on 1 Jan. 2021 (***Securities Law***).

[34] Article 135.4 of the Securities Law.

[35] During the period 2016–2020, total investment capital made by State-owned enterprises accounted for 24.5% of the total investment capital of enterprises of all types (pp. 42–43) but their net revenues represent only 14.2% of the net revenues of companies of all types (pp. 42–43 and 45–46 of the White Book of Vietnamese Companies 2022, available at https://www.gso.gov.vn/wp-content/uploads/2022/11/Sach-trang-DN-2022.pdf).

[36] According to a decree of the Government, all SOEs should have been converted into LLCs or JSCs by 1 Jul. 2010 and should now operate under the Enterprise Law. It is not clear how many SOEs have failed to meet this deadline. Numerous SOEs have not yet equitised (i.e., no interests have yet been sold to third parties).

[37] The Law on Cooperatives of the National Assembly dated 20 Nov. 2012.

[38] A business cooperation contract does not create a separate legal entity. Telecoms ventures were originally undertaken in the form of business cooperation contracts.

contributions, they also have some fundamentally different characteristics which have consequences in the context of an acquisition:

(a) The charter capital of a JSC is divided into shares owned by an unlimited number of shareholders, but there must be at least three shareholders.[39] If the target company has less than three shareholders after an acquisition, then it would have to convert itself from a JSC into an LLC. By contrast, in LLCs, the charter capital is divided into ownership interests owned by between one and fifty members.
(b) In general, shareholders of a JSC have the right to freely transfer their shares:
   (i) If the JSC is a public company, the transfer of shares will be subject to securities regulations.
   (ii) If the public company is listed, the transfer of shares will also be subject to the rules of the relevant stock exchange and provisions of the Securities Law.
   (iii) By contrast, if an investor purchases the charter capital of an LLC, the parties must comply with the pre-emption rights of other members of the LLC.[40]
(c) Only a JSC can list on a securities exchange in Vietnam.
(d) Corporate governance of an LLC can be more flexible than that of a JSC.
(e) JSCs can issue different classes of shares, whereas LLCs do not have shares at all.
(f) Both JSCs and LLCs can issue bonds, but only JSCs can issue convertible bonds.

2.3 Compliance and Reporting Requirements: Non-public Companies

[96]

No.	*Issues*	*Joint Stock Company*	*LLC*
1.	Public announcement – registration of change of ownership[41]	Any change to information published in the corporate registry about a company must be published on the National Business Registration Portal within thirty days after the date of an amended enterprise registration certificate.[42]	

[39] Article 111.1(b) of the Enterprise Law.
[40] Article 52 of the Enterprise Law.
[41] Public companies will be subject to various public disclosure requirements set out in the Securities Law and its implementing regulations (including Circular 96/2020/TT-BTC of the MOF dated 16 Nov. 2020 on public disclosure on the stock market (***Circular 96***)).
[42] Article 32 of the Enterprise Law.

No.	*Issues*	*Joint Stock Company*	*LLC*
2.	Change of shareholding/ capital contribution	Any changes in the charter capital of a company must be registered with the licensing authority within ten days after the completion of share issuance[43] and must be recorded in the enterprise registration certificate (formerly known as the business registration certificate). If there is a change in a foreign shareholder of an unlisted company, such change must be notified to the licensing authority within ten days after the foreign shareholder is recorded in the register of shareholders of the company.[44] If there is a change in any founding shareholder of an unlisted company, such change must be notified to the licensing authority within ten days after the change.[45]	For multi-member LLCs, a change of charter capital must be notified to the relevant licensing authority within ten days after the completion of the capital contribution.[46] For a one-member LLC, if a new member contributes capital to the company, the company must apply for conversion into a multi-member LLC (and record the new member in the enterprise registration certificate with the licensing authority) within ten days from the date when the new member makes its capital contribution.[47] In addition, any changes to: (i) the charter capital or (ii) the capital contribution of a member must be recorded in the enterprise registration certificate.

[43] Article 123.4 of the Enterprise Law.

[44] Article 31.3 of the Enterprise Law and Art. 58 of Decree 01/2021/ND-CP of the Government dated 4 Jan. 2021 providing guidance on enterprise registration (***Decree 01***).

[45] Article 30.1 and 30.2 of the Enterprise Law and Art. 57 of Decree 01.

[46] Article 87.2(a) of the Enterprise Law.

[47] *Ibid*.

No.	*Issues*	*Joint Stock Company*	*LLC*
3.	Change of legal representatives	A change of a legal representative (who can be (i) for a JSC, the chairman of the board or the general director and (ii) for an LLC, the chairman of the members' council, the president or the general director, depending on the charter) must be recorded in the enterprise registration certificate and be notified to licensing authorities within ten days after the change.[48]	
4.	Change of authorised representatives	Appointment of authorised representatives of shareholding entities must be notified to the company.[49] The company must notify any change of information relating to the authorised representative(s) of a foreign shareholder of the relevant licensing authority within three working days after receipt of such notification.[50]	Appointment of authorised representatives of a member in a liability limited company must be notified to the company.[51] There is no requirement for notification to the licensing authorities of the change of an authorised representative of the owners of multi-member LLCs.
5.	Annual accounts	Audited annual financial reports of a foreign-invested company must be submitted to the relevant Tax Department, Statistics Department, Department of Finance and Department of Planning and Investment (***DPI***) within ninety days after the expiry of each fiscal year.[52]	
6.	Annual finalisation of corporate income tax (***CIT***)	Each company must finalise its CIT returns and submit an application for such finalisation to the relevant Tax Department on or before the last day of the third month after the end of each fiscal year.[53]	

[48] Article 30.2 of the Enterprise Law.

[49] Article 14.4 of the Enterprise Law.

[50] Article 176.3 of the Enterprise Law and Art. 60 of Decree 01.

[51] Article 14.4 of the Enterprise Law.

[52] Articles 109 and 110 of Circular 200/2014/TT-BTC of the MOF dated 22 Dec. 2014 (as amended on 14 Jul. 2015 and 21 Mar. 2016) providing guidance on the accounting regime for enterprises.

[53] Article 44 of Law No. 38/2019/QH14 on Tax Management of National Assembly dated 13 Jun. 2019.

2.4 Minimum Capital

[97] There are generally no minimum capital requirements for Vietnamese companies. In principle, a company is expected to have enough capital resources to realise the business goals set out in its enterprise registration certificate (and, where applicable, the investment registration certificate). In certain conditional sectors, the licensing authorities sometimes examine capital resources carefully before deciding whether or not to issue a certificate.[54]

[98] With respect to a foreign-owned company undertaking only one investment project, the authorised investment capital of the company is stated in the investment registration certificate and is composed of two elements: contributed capital, equivalent to equity, and loan capital. The foreign-owned company cannot borrow a medium- or long-term loan for a project if the total of that loan and the authorised charter capital is in excess of the authorised investment capital with respect to the project.[55]

[99] Despite the generality of the above, minimum capital requirements, usually known as 'legal capital' in Vietnam, exist in certain regulated sectors, including:

No.	*Business Lines*	*Legal Capital*[56]
1.	**Commercial banks**	VND3 000 bn[57]
2.	**Finance companies**	VND500 bn[58]
3.	**Finance leasing companies**	VND150 bn[59]

[54] The track record of the licensing authorities in predicting the ability of foreign investors to raise the capital required for their project has been less than stellar. The history of investment licensing has been littered with examples of projects that did not have, or could not raise, sufficient funds.

[55] This does not apply to companies that are not required to obtain an investment registration certificate.

[56] In this chapter, we use the exchange rate of USD1 = VND23 500.

[57] Article 2 of Decree 86/2019/ND-CP of the Government dated 14 Nov. 2019 on issuance of list of legal capital of credit institutions and branches of foreign banks (***Decree 86***). Pursuant to Decree 86, the legal capital required for a policy bank is VND5 000 bn, for a commercial bank is VND3 000 bn, for a co-operative bank is VND3 000 bn, for the people's credit fund operating within a commune or town is VND0.5 bn and for the people's credit fund operating within a ward or within an inter-commune, commune-ward and inter-ward area is VND0.1 bn.

[58] Article 2 of Decree 86.

[59] *Ibid.*

No.	Business Lines	Legal Capital[56]
4.	**Insurance**	
	Non-life insurance business	VND300–400 bn[60]
	Life insurance business	VND600–1 000 bn[61]
	Health insurance business only	VND300 bn[62]
	Insurance brokerage business	VND4–8 bn[63]
	Re-insurance business	VND 400–1 100 bn[64]
5.	**Aviation**	
	Airline/air transportation business	– To operate up to ten aircraft: VND300 bn[65] – To operate from eleven up to thirty aircraft: VND600 bn[66] – To operate more than thirty aircraft: VND700 bn[67]
	Establishment of an airline engaging in general aviation business[68] for commercial purposes	VND100 bn[69]

[60] Article 10.1 of Decree 73/2016/ND-CP of the Government dated 1 Jul. 2016 providing guidelines on the implementation of the Law on Amendment of the Law on Insurance Business (as amended on 7 Nov. 2018 and 1 Nov. 2019) (***Decree 73***).

[61] Article 10.2 of Decree 73.

[62] Article 10.3 of Decree 73.

[63] Article 10.6 of Decree 73.

[64] Article 10.4 of Decree 73.

[65] Article 8.1(a) of Decree 92/2016/ND-CP of the Government dated 1 Jul. 2016 on conditional businesses in the field of air transportation (as amended on 15 Nov. 2019 and 15 Sep. 2022) (***Decree 92***).

[66] Article 8.1(b) of Decree 92.

[67] Article 8.1(c) of Decree 92.

[68] A company engaged in general aviation activities cannot engage in the public carriage of passengers, baggage, cargo or postal items. The term relates to activities which make use of aircraft for industrial, agricultural, forestry, fishery, construction or other economic purposes, to serve search and rescue, emergency aid, salvage, health, scientific research, cultural, sport, training, coaching, testing, measurement, photographing, video-recording, and other personal and civil flight needs. Article 198 of the Law on Civil Aviation of the National Assembly dated 29 Jun. 2006 (as amended on 1 Jul. 2015) (***Law on Aviation***).

[69] Article 8.2 of Decree 92.

No.	*Business Lines*	*Legal Capital*[56]
	Airport enterprises	VND100 bn[70]
	Non-airport enterprises providing aviation services	VND30 bn[71]

2.5 Governance Structure in a Vietnamese Company

[100]

(a) A multi-member LLC must have:[72]
  - (i) a members' council consisting of all owners or authorised representatives thereof;
  - (ii) a chairman of the members' council appointed by the members' council;
  - (iii) a director or general director appointed by the members' council; and
  - (iv) a supervisory body if the LLC is a State-owned company or a subsidiary of a State-owned company.

(b) The governance structure of a one-member LLC owned by an entity can be either of the following:[73]
  - (i) a chairman of the company appointed by the owner of the company; and
  - (ii) a director or general director appointed by the owner of the company or the chairman.

  or:
  - (i) a members' council consisting of three to seven representatives appointed by the owner of the company;
  - (ii) a chairman of the members' council appointed by the owner of the company; and
  - (iii) a director or general director appointed by the owner of the company.

(c) The governance structure of a JSC can be either of the following:[74]
  - (i) a general meeting of shareholders consisting of all shareholders who have the right to vote;
  - (ii) a board consisting of between three and eleven persons appointed at a general meeting of shareholders;
  - (iii) a chairman of the board;
  - (iv) a general director appointed by the board; and

[70] Article 14.2(a) of Decree 92.
[71] Article 17 of Decree 92.
[72] Article 51 of the Enterprise Law.
[73] Article 79 of the Enterprise Law.
[74] Article 137 of the Enterprise Law.

(v) a supervisory body. A supervisory body is not required if the JSC has less than eleven shareholders and no corporate shareholder is holding 50% or more of the company's shares.

or:

(i) a general meeting of shareholders consisting of all shareholders who have the right to vote;
(ii) a board consisting of between three and eleven persons appointed at a general meeting of shareholders, with at least 20% of members of the board being independent members. Instead of having a supervisory body, the company must have an internal audit committee under the board led by independent members of the board;
(iii) a chairman of the board; and
(iv) a general director appointed by the board.

2.6 Decision-Making

(a) Decision-Making in a Multi-Member LLC

[101] The members' council is the highest decision-making body. All members of a multi-member LLC have the right to participate in the meetings of the members' council, and each has the number of votes corresponding to the capital contributed by it. The members' council normally makes decisions on major issues affecting the LLC. The decisions of the members' council are deemed to be approved at a meeting by participating members owning at least 65% of the charter capital. This rises to at least 75% of the charter capital if such decisions are related to:[75]

(i) sale of assets valued at 50% or more of the total value of assets recorded in the most recent financial statement of the company;
(ii) amendment of or addition to the charter; or
(iii) reorganisation or dissolution of the company.

[102] The law allows the charter to stipulate a different approval threshold (which can be either a higher or lower percentage).

(b) Decision-Making in a One-Member LLC

[103] If a one-member LLC has a members' council, then (unless otherwise stipulated in the charter of the company) a resolution of the members' council is passed when agreed by more than 50% of the attending members. This rises to at least 75% of the attending members if such decisions are related to:[76]

(i) an amendment of or addition to the charter of the company; or
(ii) a reorganisation of the company; or

[75] Article 59 of the Enterprise Law.
[76] Article 80.6 of the Enterprise Law.

(iii) a transfer of a part or all of the charter capital of the company.

[104] If a one-member LLC is run by the chairman (a.k.a president) rather than a members' council, as is possible in a one-member company, the chairman acts on behalf of the owner to perform all rights and obligations of the owner. Unless the company charter provides otherwise, the chairman is the highest decision-making person in the company.

(c) Decision-Making in a JSC

[105] The general meeting of shareholders of a JSC is the highest decision-making body in such a company. All ordinary shareholders have the right to participate in the general meeting of shareholders, each with the number of votes corresponding to the ordinary shares held. The general meeting of shareholders normally makes decisions only on major issues affecting the company. However, its power can be extended by the shareholders in any manner that is incorporated in the charter. As a general rule, resolutions of the general meeting of shareholders are passed when approved by shareholders representing more than 50% of the total voting shares of all attending shareholders. This rises to at least 65% for certain specific issues, including:[77]

(i) classes of shares and the total number of shares of each class to be offered;
(ii) amendment to the business lines of the company;
(iii) change of company's organisational structure;
(iv) investments or sale of assets equal to or more than 35% of the total value of assets recorded in the latest financial statements of the company or a smaller percentage set out in the charter;
(v) restructuring or dissolution of the company; and
(vi) other cases defined by the charter.

[106] The law allows the charter to stipulate a higher (but not lower) approval percentage.

[107] The board decides important matters not falling within the authority of the general meeting of shareholders. Unless the charter provides for a higher voting threshold, the Board makes decisions by a simple majority of votes.[78] The chairman will have a casting vote.[79]

2.7 Executive Authority

[108] A general director or director is the highest executive in the company and is responsible for the day-to-day management of the business of the company.

[77] Article 148.1 of the Enterprise Law.
[78] Article 157.12 of the Enterprise Law.
[79] *Ibid.*

2.8 Legal Representative

[109] All Vietnamese companies must have at least one legal representative. A JSC and an LLC can have more than one legal representative.[80] If a company has more than one legal representative, its charter must specifically set out the rights and obligations of each legal representative; otherwise, each legal representative shall be deemed to be a lawful legal representative vis-a-vis a third party, and all of the legal representatives are jointly liable for any damage caused to the company.[81]

[110] The legal representatives of a company have broad powers and responsibilities, including representing the company before the courts and governmental agencies, and executing all agreements with third parties unless the law provides otherwise.[82]

[111] Companies must have at least one legal representative who resides in Vietnam.[83] If a company has only one legal representative and they are overseas for a period of thirty consecutive days, they must give a power of attorney to another person.[84]

2.9 Foreign Management

[112]

(a) There are no restrictions on the number of foreign directors that can sit on the board of a Vietnamese JSC. There are, however, limits to the size of a board in the law, and possibly also in the company's charter.
(b) Foreign managers usually need to obtain work permits. Obtaining such work permits is a cumbersome process. Exemptions are available for, amongst other cases, the following:[85]
  (i) owners of an LLC which has charter capital of VND3 m or more;
  (ii) chairman or members of the board of a JSC which has charter capital of VND3 m or more;
  (iii) head of a representative office/project or the person in charge of the operation of an international organisation or a foreign non-governmental organisation in Vietnam;
  (iv) people working in Vietnam for a period of less than three months in certain situations;
  (v) foreign lawyers who have been granted lawyer's practising certificates in Vietnam in accordance with the Law on Lawyers;

---

[80] Article 12.2 of the Enterprise Law.

[81] *Ibid.*

[82] Article 12.1 of the Enterprise Law; Article 139.1 of Law on 91/2015/QH13 on Civil Code of the National Assembly of Vietnam dated 24 Nov. 2015 (***Civil Code***).

[83] Article 12.3 of the Enterprise Law.

[84] Article 12.5 of the Enterprise Law.

[85] Article 154 of the Labour Code of the National Assembly dated 20 Nov. 2019 (***Labour Code***) and Art. 7 of Decree 152/2020/ND-CP of the Government dated 30 Dec. 2020 providing guidance on a number of articles of the Labour Code on foreign employees working in Vietnam (***Decree 152***).

(vi) people working in accordance with provisions of an international treaty of which Vietnam is a member;
(vii) internal transferees within an enterprise and within the scope of the list of commitments on services of Vietnam within the WTO;
(viii) foreigners who are married to Vietnamese citizens and have been residing in Vietnam.
At law, a foreigner who is exempt from obtaining a work permit may still need to conduct procedures to confirm the exemption.[86]

(c) The legal representative of a company must permanently reside in Vietnam if the company has only one legal representative.[87] In addition, more than half of the members of the supervisory board[88] of a JSC must permanently reside in Vietnam.

(d) There is generally no requirement for the presence of officials in the management of a Vietnamese company. The exception is for certain large enterprises which are partly owned by the State, where the representative of the capital owned by the State tends to be a State official.

3 REGULATORY FRAMEWORK

3.1 Laws Affecting Acquisitions

(a) Principal Laws

[113] The legal framework for mergers and acquisitions remains underdeveloped. There is no single law governing acquisitions in Vietnam:

(i) The main rules are contained in the Enterprise Law, which governs companies, and the Investment Law, which governs investments by or in companies generally.
(ii) The Securities Law and its implementing regulations, in particular Decree 155,[89] regulate the acquisitions of shares of a public company in Vietnam, including public tender offers (***PTOs***). The rules of the stock exchange could also impact an acquisition of a public company if it is listed.
(iii) In addition to the general company and investment rules, the acquisition of shares in a Vietnamese company operating in some sectors, such as banking, financial services and insurance, is regulated by sector-specific legislation.[90]

---

[86] Article 8 of Decree 152.

[87] Article 12.3 of the Enterprise Law.

[88] Article 168.2 of the Enterprise Law.

[89] Decree 155/2020/ND-CP of the Government dated 31 Dec. 2020 providing details and guiding implementation of the Securities Law (***Decree 155***).

[90] For example, the purchase of shares in Vietnamese credit institutions by foreign investors is governed by Decree 01/2014/ND-CP of the Government dated 3 Jan. 2014 on foreign investors acquiring shares in Vietnamese credit institutions.

(iv) Acquisitions of interests in State-owned companies, either during or after their equitisation, are governed by separate sets of regulations.[91]

(b) Principal Variables

[114] Within this framework, the relevant principles will depend on whether the transaction is onshore or offshore, the nature of the Vietnamese company that is being acquired, and the type of transaction that is being envisaged. There are several main categories:

(i) Entirely offshore transactions indirectly affecting the ownership of companies in Vietnam.
(ii) Acquisitions of any percentage of a company operating in a regulated sector or a sector subject to international commitments such as WTO commitments.
(iii) Acquisitions of interests in public companies.
(iv) Acquisitions of non-public Vietnamese companies which are not within sections 3.1(b)(ii) and 3.1(b)(iii) above.
(v) Acquisitions of strategic interests in current or former SOEs.[92]
(vi) Asset purchases.
(vii) Mergers.

3.2 Relevant Regulatory Authorities

[115] Many governmental authorities could be relevant to an acquisition in Vietnam.

(a) Government

[116] The Government is the highest executive body in Vietnam.[93] The head of the Government is the Prime Minister, who is assisted by a number of Deputy Prime Ministers. The Government will be relevant to any sale involving a substantial State-owned company, particularly in an equitisation. It will also be the entity that makes the final decision on matters that cannot be resolved by the line ministries and on any sensitive matters.

(b) Central-Level Ministries

[117] Ministries of the Government will take decisions involving State companies for which they have oversight. For example, the MOIT is in charge of State management of, among other things, commercial and domestic markets, electronic commerce, competition, consumer protection, electricity and oil and gas.[94] So, if there is an acquisition of an interest in an oil and gas project, such as the Southwest

[91] *See* discussion in section 'Acquisitions in the State Sector'.

[92] *Ibid.*

[93] Law on Organisation of the Government of the National Assembly dated 19 Jun. 2015 (as amended on 1 Jul. 2020).

[94] Decree 96/2022/ND-CP of the Government dated 29 Nov. 2022 providing functions, tasks, powers and organisation structure of the Ministry of Industry and Trade.

gas–to–power project running from Blocks B/52 to O Mon/Kien Giang, it would have to be approved by the MOIT.[95]

(c) Ministry of Planning and Investment (*MPI*)

[118] The MPI is responsible for the management of foreign investment in Vietnam.[96] It is the channel through which applications are made for projects requiring investment policy decisions from the National Assembly or the Prime Minister. It resolves ambiguities in the laws and regulations relating to investment (of which there are numerous). It, therefore, has the final say (not always exercised) if a provincial DPI cannot decide how to act in a specific situation. It should also resolve inconsistencies between provinces in the application of laws and regulations as applied to foreign investments, but it does not always do so. If an investment project has an investment registration certificate that was issued or amended improperly or illegally, the MPI can make recommendations regarding its suspension.

(d) Provincial People's Committee and Department of Planning and Investment (*DPI*)

[119] In each province, there is a people's committee that is the highest executive body. The DPI is the body to which it delegates the task of licensing foreign investment. For most foreign acquisitions, this is the key governmental body.

(e) State Securities Commission (*SSC*)

[120] The SSC manages the securities market and the stock exchanges as well as the approvals and licences needed for acquisitions of securities-companies, funds and fund management companies[97] and certain transactions involving shares of public companies.

(f) State Bank of Vietnam (*SBV*)

[121] The SBV has the power to manage and approve acquisitions of banks and non-bank financial institutions.

(g) Vietnam Securities Depositary (*VSD*)

[122] The VSD is in charge of the registration, depository, clearing, and settlement of securities and providing services supporting securities transactions in respect of securities registered and deposited at the VSD.[98]

---

95 By virtue of Decree 95/2015/ND-CP of the Government dated 16 Oct. 2015 implementing the Petroleum Law, as amended, the MOIT replaced the MPI as the authority in charge of issuing the amended investment certificate approving transfers of participating interests in Petroleum Sharing Contracts.

96 Decree 89/2022/ND-CP of the Government dated 28 Oct. 2022 providing functions, tasks, powers and organisation structure of the MPI.

97 Decree 48/2015/QĐ-TTg of the Government dated 8 Oct. 2015 providing functions, tasks, powers and organisation structure of the State Securities Commission.

98 Article 9 of Decision 171/2008/QĐ-TTg of the Prime Minister dated 18 Dec. 2008 on establishment of the Vietnam Securities Depositary (VSD). Pursuant to Art. 52 of the Securities Law and Decision 26/2022/QĐ-TTg of the Prime Minister dated 16 Dec. 2022, Viet Nam Securities Depository and

(h) Vietnam Competition Authority

[123] The Vietnam Competition Commission (***VCC***), a body under the MOIT, has jurisdiction over merger control and competition issues.[99]

3.3 Regulatory Framework

[124] The approval/registration procedures applicable to foreign acquisition of a private company depend on the type of acquisition involved:

(a) If (1) one of the authorised business lines of the target is subject to market access conditions (*see* section 'Acquisition of companies engaged in businesses that are subject to conditions) and the foreign ownership of the target increases as a result of the acquisition, (2) the acquisition results in an increase of foreign ownership to more than 50% of the charter capital, or (3) a foreign investor acquires an interest in a target company having land in certain border, coastal or national defence or security locations,[100] there is a two-step procedure:
   (i) The acquisition has to be registered, and an approval notice has to be obtained from the licensing authority. Such approval should be issued within fifteen days from the receipt of a 'valid' application dossier in cases (1) and (2) above. Ten additional working days are allowed in respect of (3) above;[101] and
   (ii) upon approval, the change of ownership has to be registered. In theory, this should take three working days after the file has been submitted.[102]

(b) For other cases, the only obligation in relation to foreign investment is to register the change of ownership.[103]

(c) The target company is obliged to comply with certain reporting obligations set out in the section 'Compliance and reporting requirements' above.

Clearing Corporation (VSDC) will be established to replace the VSD. At the time of preparing this article the VSDC has not been established yet. Once the VSDC is established, it will take over all the functions of the VSD as such all references to VSD herein will be deemed to refer to VSDC.

99 *See* discussion in section 'Merger Control'.

100 Article 26 of the Investment Law No. 61/2020/QH14 of the National Assembly dated 17 Jun. 2020 (the ***Investment Law***). 'National defence or security locations' are vaguely referred to so that any case that the target has the land may be potentially subject to two steps procedure.

101 Article 66.3 and 66.4 of Decree 31/2021/ND-CP of the Government dated 26 Mar. 2021 guiding the implementation of the Investment Law (***Decree 31***).

102 Statutory time periods tend not to mean much and start running from the day that the authority accepts (in its discretion) that the application file is complete.

103 If the target company is an LLC, an amendment to the enterprise registration certificate reflecting changes of the company's owners will be required (Art. 28 of the Enterprise Law). If the target company is a JSC, an amendment is only required if there is a change of founding shareholders (Art. 31.1(b) of the Enterprise Law), a change of foreign investors in a non-listed company (Art. 31.1(b) of the Enterprise Law) or if the acquisition results in an increase or decrease of the charter capital of the company (Art. 30.1 of the Enterprise Law).

(d) If the target company increases the charter capital as a result of the investment of the investor, it will need to update the enterprise registration certificate to record the new charter capital within ten days after the increase.[104]
(e) If the target company is a foreign-invested company, it may have an investment registration certificate in respect of its investment project.[105] The change of ownership of the target company may require an amendment to the investment registration certificate to record the buyer as an investor in the investment project undertaken by the target company.[106]

[125] The approval/registration procedures applicable to foreign acquisition of a public company are set out in the section 'Public Company Acquisitions'.

[126] In theory, the role of the authorities should be limited to checking and confirming whether or not the proposed acquisition is subject to any conditions and, if so, whether it is in line with the applicable conditions. They should conduct the requested registration if the proposed investment meets the required conditions.

3.4 Acquisition of Companies Engaged in Businesses that are Subject to Conditions

(a) General Rules

[127] Regardless of its intended ownership interest, a foreign investor has to work through three main lists in order to know how its potential acquisition will be treated:

(i) First, the list of prohibited businesses in which no investment is permitted.[107]
(ii) Second, the list of conditional businesses which specifies investments that are permitted but subject to conditions.[108]
(iii) Third, the list of so-called market access conditions, only applicable to foreign investors, is a list of businesses where foreigners are not allowed to access the market yet or where market access is permitted but subject to conditions (such as conditions on the foreign investor's ownership interest, the investment method, the scope of investment and the capacity of the investor).[109]

104 Article 30 of the Enterprise Law. If the target company is an LLC, the enterprise registration certificate must be amended to record the ownership of the members.
105 Article 37 of the Investment Law.
106 Article 66.6 of Decree 31 is silent on the requirement on amendment of the investment registration certificate, but it requires the target company to register the change of members/shareholders with the DPI in compliance with the business registration regulations. Rights and obligations of the foreign investors as the members/shareholders in the target company will be established upon the completion of the change of members/shareholders.
107 The list of prohibited business is set out under Art. 6 of the Investment Law. It includes, for example, business in some types of chemicals or minerals. This applies to both domestic investors and foreign investors.
108 Article 7 and Annex IV of the Investment Law.
109 Article 9 of the Investment Law and Annex I of Decree 31.

(b) Conditional Businesses

[128] There are two lists of conditional business lines, namely (i) the list of conditional business lines; and (ii) the list of market access conditions applicable to foreign investors.

[129] The Investment Law contains a list of 227 conditional business lines, compared with 243 conditional business lines in the 2014 Investment Law.[110] Both foreign and local investors are subject to these conditions.

[130] The market access conditions are listed in Decree 31 and cover 25 business lines that foreigners are not allowed to access and 59 business lines where conditions will apply to foreigners (i.e., 'market access conditions'). The MPI is responsible for consolidating these market access conditions and uploading them onto a national investment portal.[111] The list of market access conditions applicable to foreign investors contains the type of condition that is applicable to the area or type of investment:[112]

(i) a foreign ownership limit might be applicable to an investment in certain sectors;
(ii) there might be conditions on the form that the investment can take (e.g., a joint venture may be required);
(iii) there might be conditions on the scope of the investment (e.g., some educational businesses are limited to teaching technical, scientific, business, economics, accounting, international law and language subjects);
(iv) there might be qualifications applicable to the investors (e.g., investors supplying facilities-based telecommunications services have to be telecommunications service suppliers duly licensed in Vietnam); and
(v) there might be other conditions set out by law or arising through a treaty to which Vietnam is a party (e.g., foreign-invested distribution companies are not allowed to distribute cigarettes and cigars, books, newspapers and magazines, video records on whatever medium, precious metals and stones, pharmaceutical products and drugs, explosives, processed oil and crude oil, rice, cane and beet sugar).[113]

(c) Acquisitions of Companies Operating in Both Conditional and Other Sectors

[131] If a foreign investor wishes to acquire a business that is engaged in various sectors, it will be obliged to meet all investment conditions applicable to each sector. As a result, if there are various foreign ownership limits applicable to different

[110] Annex 4 of the Investment Law.

[111] Article 18 of Decree 31.

[112] Article 9.3 of the Investment Law.

[113] The special laws that apply to the sector could contain any number of specific requirements. For example, for foreign investments in the distribution sector the MOIT consent is still a hurdle in practice. This can make it difficult to purchase a Vietnamese company that has more than one retail outlet. And even if the acquisition proceeds, the establishment of any additional retail outlet by the company after it becomes foreign-owned would be subject to satisfaction of the economic needs test (ENT).

businesses conducted by the target company, the acquisition will only be possible if it is of less than the lowest applicable foreign ownership limit. Alternatively, if it is possible as a business matter, the target company can amend its scope of business to remove the restricted businesses and/or divest or spin off the restricted business that causes a deal-related problem before the transfer of shares to foreign investors.

3.5 Foreign Ownership Limits

(a) Foreign Ownership Limits: Non-Public Companies

[132] Foreign investors in a non-public company should be treated as domestic investors unless they invest in sectors subject to 'market access conditions'. The foreign ownership limit applicable to a foreign-owned non-public company will be determined according to the following principles (among others):[114]

(i) if Vietnam makes no commitments under international treaties and Vietnamese laws are silent about market access conditions applicable to foreign investors, no foreign ownership limitations apply to foreign investors;[115]

(ii) if Vietnam makes no commitments under international treaties and Vietnamese laws provide for any foreign ownership limitation applicable to foreign investors, the foreign ownership limitation under Vietnamese law will apply to foreign investors;[116]

(iii) if the foreign investor is subject to an international treaty that provides for more favourable market access conditions than Vietnamese law, the market access conditions under that international treaty will apply;[117]

(iv) foreign investors are entitled to commitments of Vietnam under the WTO even if they are not from a country or territory being a WTO member;[118]

(v) foreign investors who are subject to different market access conditions under different international treaties are able to choose to apply the market access conditions under (only) one of the treaties for all of its registered business lines;[119]

(vi) if multiple foreign investors hold interests in a company and the foreign investors are subject to one or more international treaties, then the foreign ownership limit for that company cannot exceed the highest percentage permitted in any of the international treaties regulating foreign ownership.[120]

---

[114] Article 17 of Decree 31.
[115] Article 17.4(a) of Decree 31.
[116] Article 17.4(b) of Decree 31.
[117] Article 17.8 of Decree 31.
[118] Article 17.7 of Decree 31.
[119] Article 17.9 of Decree 31. Vietnam is a party to a number of multilateral and bilateral international treaties amongst which its commitments on market access conditions for foreign investors may vary significantly. Key international treaties include WTO, CPTPP, AFAS, EVFTA, VJEPA and VKFTA.
[120] Article 17.10(a) of Decree 31.

(b) Foreign Ownership Limits: Public Companies

[133] Foreign investors in a public company are permitted to hold up to 100%, except for the following:[121]

(i) *Limits under international treaties*: If the public company engages in a business activity in respect of which foreign ownership has been agreed in an international treaty to which Vietnam is a party, then this treaty will be applied (even if it is not technically a cap).[122] For instance, Vietnam's WTO commitments contain agreements in respect of various business activities, such as maritime transport services (49%), container handling services (50%), and road transportation (51%).

(ii) *Limits under sector-specific laws*: If the public company engages in a business activity that is subject to a foreign ownership cap in a sector-specific law, such cap will be applied. *See* section 'Examples of Foreign Ownership Limits'.

(iii) *Limits applied to market access conditions*: If the public company engages in a business in which a market access condition applies to foreign investors:
   (a) if Vietnamese law stipulates a foreign ownership cap, such cap will be applied; or
   (b) if Vietnamese law does not specify the foreign ownership cap for such business, the foreign ownership limit will be 50%.[123]

(iv) If the public company engages in various businesses subject to market access conditions stipulating a foreign ownership cap, the investor's ownership must not be higher than the lowest foreign ownership allowed for any business line.

(v) *Limits under equitisation regulations*: If the public company is an equitised SOE, the foreign ownership may be limited by the equitisation plan approved by the relevant governmental body at the time of equitisation.

(vi) *Limits under the charter*: A public company can impose a lower foreign ownership cap than those mentioned in (i)-(iii) by specifying such a limit in its charter. However, this must be approved by the general meeting of shareholders of such public company.

[134] Each public company should determine its own foreign ownership limit and report the same to the SSC with supporting documents. The SSC will then confirm the receipt of the complete dossier and inform the VSD accordingly.[124]

(c) Examples of Foreign Ownership Limits

[135] Some of the main sectors where there are foreign ownership restrictions and other conditions are set out below:

[121] Article 139 of Decree 155.
[122] Article 139.1(a) of Decree 155.
[123] Article 139.1(c) of Decree 155.
[124] Article 142 of Decree 155.

Sectors	*Foreign Ownership Limit*	*Other Conditions*
Banking services	*Under domestic law:*[125] (1) Any foreign individual: not to exceed 5% (2) Any foreign organisation: not to exceed 15% (3) Any foreign strategic investor: not to exceed 20% (4) Any foreign organisation and related parties: not to exceed 20% (5) Total foreign ownership in a Vietnamese bank: not to exceed 30% (6) Total foreign ownership in a Vietnamese non-bank credit institution (such as a finance company): 49%. *Under the WTO, AFAS, EVFTA:* Vietnam may restrict foreign investors in Vietnamese banks to 30%.	The restrictions described in items 2, 3, 5 and 6 would not apply if the Prime Minister authorises a different percentage ownership for the purpose of restructuring a weak credit institution or ensuring the safety of the banking system.[126] If a foreign investor wishes to avail itself of this exemption from the normal limitations, it must prepare and submit its proposal to the SBV for it to evaluate prior to referring it to the Prime Minister for approval. A buyer must meet various requirements. For example, a foreign strategic investor must have total assets of USD20 bn. A foreign investor that is not strategic and that wishes to purchase 10% or more will need to have total assets of at least USD10 bn (applicable to banks, financial institutions or financial leasing institutions) or USD1 bn (applicable to other organisations). The SBV approval would be required if the foreign investor (i) owned 5% or more of the shares of the credit institution; or (ii) became a foreign strategic investor.

[125] Decree 01/2014/ND-CP of the Government dated 3 Jan. 2014 on the purchase of shares in Vietnamese credit institutions by foreign investors.

Sectors	Foreign Ownership Limit	Other Conditions
		A buyer would be subject to certain lock-ups: (i) Five-year lock-up for foreign strategic shareholders; and (ii) Institutional foreign shareholders who own 10% or more of a credit institution are prohibited from transferring their shares for three years after the date that they reach the 10% ownership position.
Petroleum	Various limitations, depending on the specific business.	
Civil Aviation[127]	*Under domestic law:* For airlines or companies providing aviation services: 34% for all foreign investors.[128] *Under the CPTPP:* For air transportation: 30%	A single foreign investor cannot hold more than 34% of the charter capital of a company providing aviation services. The largest shareholder in a foreign-invested domestic airline must be a Vietnamese company that has no 'foreign-invested capital'. If a shareholder in a domestic airline itself has a foreign shareholder, then a pro-rata portion of the shareholding of the shareholder in the

[126] According to public information, this has occurred in practice in the context of a proposed purchase of GP Bank by United Overseas Bank.

[127] The Vietnam domestic aviation market has six air carriers, namely Vietnam Airlines (the national carrier), Jetstar Pacific Airlines (a Vietnam Airlines subsidiary), Vasco (Vietnam Air Service Company, also a subsidiary of Vietnam Airlines), and three private airlines, namely Vietjet Air, Bamboo Airways and Viettravel Airlines.

[128] Article 110.2 of the Law on Aviation and Art. 8.3(a) of Decree 92.

Sectors	*Foreign Ownership Limit*	*Other Conditions*
		domestic airline will be deemed to be owned by a foreign shareholder.
Land Transportation	*Under domestic law* 51% (transportation of goods)[129] *Under the WTO commitments* 49% (transportation of people)[130] 51% (transportation of goods)[131] *Under the AFAS* Foreign ownership not exceeding 70%	No specific conditions for foreign-owned companies.
Logistics	*Under domestic law* Sea transportation: 49%[132] Container handling: 50%[133] Customs clearance and brokerage: no cap, but must be in the form of a joint venture with a Vietnamese investor.[134] *Under the WTO* Same as domestic law	Depending on the specific business.

129 Article 4.3(g) of Decree 163/2017/ND-CP of the Government dated 30 Dec. 2017 on logistics business (***Decree 163***).

130 Section II.11.F of Schedule CLX – Vietnam to the WTO Working Party Report.

131 Article 4.3(g) of Decree 163.

132 Article 4.3(a) of Decree 163.

133 Article 4.3(b) and (c) of Decree 163.

134 Article 4.3(d) and (đ) of Decree 163.

Sectors	*Foreign Ownership Limit*	*Other Conditions*
Distribution and Retail	*Under domestic law and the WTO* Prohibited for certain goods such as cigarettes, publications, medicines, crude oil, etc. No limitation on most goods.	A foreign-invested company engaged in distribution must apply for a business licence. In addition, a foreign-invested company engaged in the retail business must apply for a licence to open each new outlet after the first one, and the opening of such outlet is conditional upon the satisfaction of an ENT.[135]
Advertisement	No cap, but must be in the form of a joint venture with a Vietnamese company authorised to engage in the advertising business.[136]	
Publishing	*Under domestic law* 0% for publishing activities.[137] Unlimited for printing and importing activities in relation to publications.[138] *Under the VJEPA* No restriction.	
Press	Highly controlled, foreign investors are generally prohibited.[139]	

[135] Decree 09/2018/ND-CP of the Government dated 15 Jan. 2018 providing detailed guidance on implementation of the Commercial Law and the Law on Foreign Trade in relation to commercial activities of foreign-owned companies. The ENT requirement will be phased out in five years after the effective date of the CPTPP and EVFTA.

[136] Section II.1.F of Schedule CLX – Vietnam to the WTO Working Party Report.

[137] Article 12 of the Law on Publishing of the National Assembly dated 20 Nov. 2012, as amended on 1 Jan. 2019 (***Publishing Law***).

[138] Article 32 of the Publishing Law.

[139] Appendix 1 to Decree 31/.

Sectors	*Foreign Ownership Limit*	*Other Conditions*
Education	*Under domestic law and treaties* 100% applicable to schools for short-term training, kindergartens (for foreign children living in Vietnam), primary and secondary schools (for foreign and Vietnamese students), vocational schools and universities.[140]	The percentage of Vietnamese students in a kindergarten or primary/secondary/high school is limited to 50%.[141] There are no limitations at vocational schools and universities. Minimum investment capital and infrastructure requirements apply for each level of education and training.
Healthcare	N/a	Minimum investment capital for each hospital is USD20 m, and for each polyclinic is USD2 m.[142]
Military-owned companies[143]	Major state-owned companies under the ownership of the Ministry of National Defence will remain wholly owned by the State.	The State may sell interests in certain military-owned companies with no military business.

3.6 Control

(a) Majority Ownership

[136] If a buyer wishes to have control of a company, they will need to determine the level of ownership that gives them the desired control. Shareholder issues require approval by more than 50% of all the votes of shareholders attending a meeting or by at least 65% of all the votes of shareholders attending a meeting in respect of more serious corporate matters.[144] Board control can normally be

[140] Decree 86/2018/ND-CP of the Government dated 6 Jun. 2018 on foreign investment in the field of education (*Decree 86*).

[141] Article 39 of Decree 86.

[142] Section II.8 of Schedule CLX – Vietnam to the WTO Working Party Report.

[143] Official Correspondence 1604/TTg-DMDN of the Prime Minister dated 8 Oct. 2013.

[144] Article 148 of the Enterprise Law. *See* discussion in section 'Governance Structure in a Vietnamese Company' for further details.

achieved with more than 50% interest as long as the acquisition documentation and charter are appropriately drafted (*see* below).

[137] In a multi-member LLC, an ordinary resolution requires a 65% vote to pass (and 75% for resolutions on certain serious matters). Members can, however, agree to a lower percentage if they so stipulate in the company's charter.

(b) Practice

[138] Pursuant to the Enterprise Law, a shareholder or a group of shareholders must own 10% of a company to be able to nominate directors to the board.[145] However, the charter of the company can provide a lower percentage. Investors should check the threshold in the charter of the target company or negotiate with the sellers in relation to this threshold if it would affect their potential rights after a transaction.

[139] In addition, acquirers need to be aware that:

(i) the board of a Vietnamese company is appointed for a term of up to five years. Unless the incumbent directors resign or the size of the board is increased, there may be no vacancies for the appointment of new directors nominated by the new shareholder; and
(ii) unless otherwise provided in the charter, the board will be elected by cumulative voting, in which each shareholder has a number of votes calculated by multiplying the number of shares it holds by the number of directors to be elected to the board; a shareholder can choose to use these votes to support the election of multiple directors (by apportioning them) or can vote them all in favour of just one candidate; and directors are elected on the basis of the highest number of votes received.

[140] The above means that an investor may not be able to secure the majority of the board of the target company for some years, even if it acquires more than 50% of such company. Investors should, therefore, require the sellers to procure the appointment of directors nominated by them as a condition precedent to closing or a closing deliverable.

3.7 Timing of Governmental Approvals: Practical Considerations

[141] The timing and procedures for obtaining governmental approval are set out in the relevant laws. However, in practice, the governmental authorities normally have broad discretion in reviewing and approving an application file. Therefore, the real time required to obtain governmental approval is rarely clear in advance.

[142] In general, governmental entities would not need to take action on any application until the application file is deemed 'complete'. The word 'complete' gives the DPI, MPI, MOIT or other relevant approving entity ample opportunity to take as long as it needs to process the application. There is an additional

[145] Article 115.4 of the Enterprise Law.

complication in complex or sensitive cases, as the file would probably not be deemed complete until it contains the approval from a higher-level authority or line ministry, which in some cases may be the Prime Minister.[146] The amount of time taken by such authority, line ministry, or the Prime Minister to respond in such cases is unpredictable.

[143] Assuming a straight transfer of shares of a Vietnamese company, without any attempt on the part of the buyer to change the investment registration certificate for other purposes (such as to add rights or business lines), it could take two to three months after the deal is signed to put the documents together and secure an acquisition approval and the amended enterprise registration certificate. The actual amount of time required will depend on numerous factors, including:

(a) the nature of the business involved and the conditions applicable to foreign investment in it;
(b) the relationships that the seller (and the buyer) has with the DPI and other relevant bodies;
(c) the identity of the buyer and the amount of effort that such buyer puts into developing the relevant relationships during the purchase process and into resolving any issues of concern prior to submitting the documents (i.e., while the deal is being negotiated);
(d) the political and business sensitivity of the transfer; and
(e) (in some unfortunate cases) the desire of competitors to prevent the transaction from completing.

[144] In abnormal cases, the time required to obtain approvals can be very long indeed.

[145] The investors may choose (themselves or through advisors) to follow up actively with the relevant licensing authorities, such as the DPI, to attempt to expedite the process. This could involve, for example, discussing pending issues, the requirements of the authorities and how to satisfy them. However, there is usually no guarantee that such work will be effective, at least in any specific time frame.

3.8 Acquisitions of Interests Through Nominees

[146] While nominee arrangements are not uncommon in Vietnam, there is no concept of a 'trust' under Vietnamese law. As a result, nominee arrangements come in various forms in practice. Often, they involve undertakings from the nominee, service agreements with the nominee, loan agreements, call option agreements,

[146] By way of background, the application file will go through the Office of the Government which is the office that supports the Prime Minister and the Cabinet. It is composed of numerous departments. It operates above the ministries such as the MPI that are otherwise responsible for foreign investment.

equity mortgage agreements and proxy agreements.[147] In situations where the foreign party has valuable rights offshore, there may also be a licence agreement enabling the nominee company to use such rights in Vietnam. In the context of sectors that are not considered sensitive, the risk of such arrangements being investigated and unwound is not high because the authorities tend not to view arrangements as a whole but to see each element of the arrangement as a discreet transaction.

[147] While the regulators may seldom act of their own volition, it is always possible that they could be stirred into action by another business seeking to thwart a competitor or, indeed, by a dissatisfied nominee. If the authorities do investigate, and become aware of nominee arrangements, then in the absence of specific permission for a nominee arrangement (which is unlikely), they could declare the transaction to be void.[148]

[148] In addition, the nominee, holding the legal title, could assert that it has ownership of the company, as the beneficial nominee arrangement would not be enforceable in Vietnam.

[149] Some relatively straightforward structuring steps are being used to sidestep the foreign ownership limitation, as the 54% Thai Beverage purchase of Saigon Beer Company (Sabeco) demonstrated.

[150] The above Sabeco structure requires the involvement of local investors. In practice, some foreign investors are employing the following multi-layer structure, which does not require any local investors.

---

147 Many commentators take the view that the Sabeco arrangement, which seems to have been blessed by the State authorities of Vietnam, was effectively a nominee arrangement.

148 The Investment Law specifically provides that an investment project can be terminated if the investor conducts investment activities on the basis of a false transaction. Article 48.2(e) of the Investment Law.

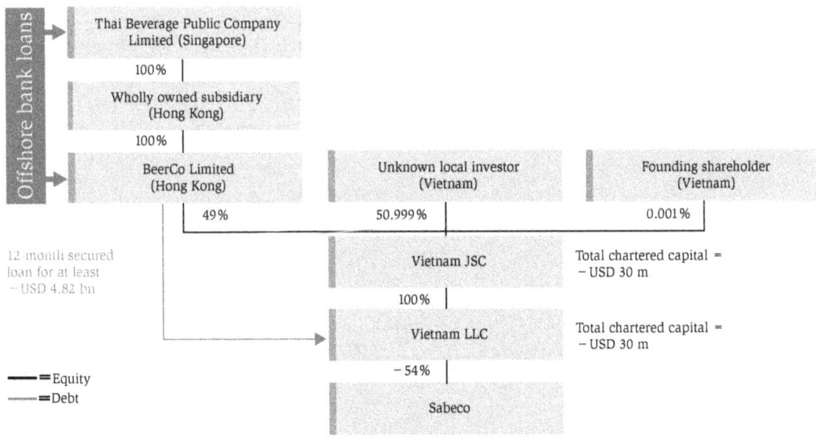

In 2017, the government successfully sold a 54% stake in Sabeco, the largest brewer in Vietnam, for roughly USD 5 bn.

**Sabeco is subject to a foreign ownership limit of 49%.
Prior to the auction, foreigners already owned ~10% of Sabeco, meaning that the stake available to a foreign investor was limited to ~39%.**

In Vietnam, a Vietnamese incorporated company is treated as foreign if foreigners own more than 49% of the company.

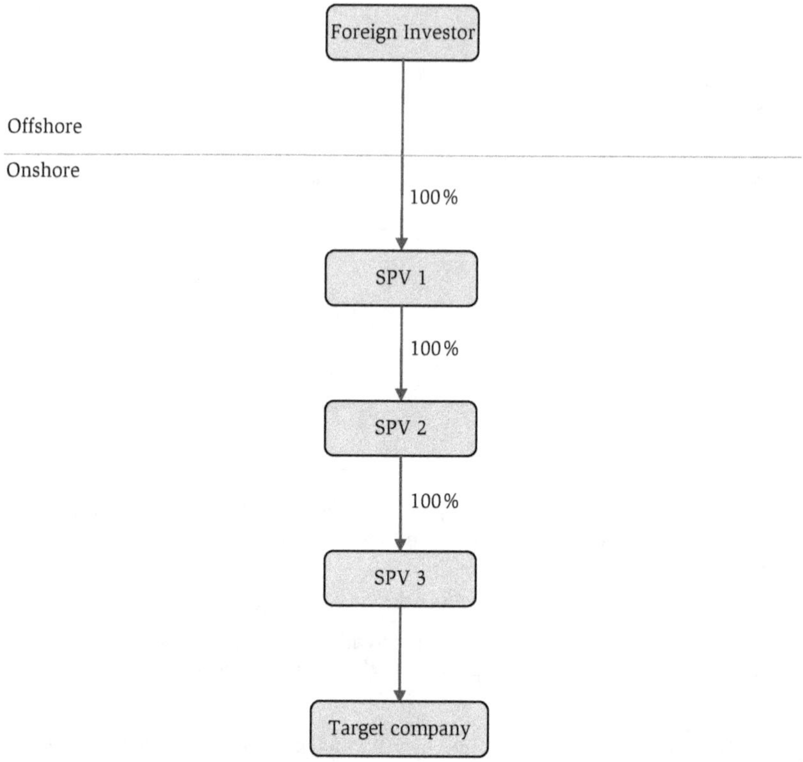

[151] This multi-layer structure is however subject to a high risk that the authorities may 'look through' the SPVs and deem the foreign investor to be ultimately holding the interest in the target company.

4 ACQUISITIONS IN THE STATE SECTOR

4.1 Disposals by the State: Prognosis

[152] Some strategic investors buy minority interests in SOEs in the hope of increasing their ownership stake over the course of time, either through the exercise of options that they negotiate at the time of initial purchase or through the exercise of rights of first refusal that are not taken up by other shareholders in a capital increase. These rights are not available in respect of all SOEs and are subject to ownership limitations set out in the law. The State has also determined that it will not sell some companies in certain sectors and will not sell more than a stated percentage of companies in other sectors. The State has recently shown its increasing reluctance to divest from SOEs.

[153] Based on recent decisions by the Prime Minister, the State intends its ownership of SOEs to be as set out below:[149]

- **No sales of State Interests** – The State will retain 100% ownership in sectors of national interest, such as cartography for national defence and public security; manufacturing and trading in industrial explosives and supply blasting services; publishing; transportation safety; lotteries; companies operating inter-provincial and inter-district irrigation works; applying high technology and large investment or creating a driving force for rapid development for other industries and the economy; constructing and operating large power plants that have especially significant socio-economic, national defence and public security positions; oil and gas exploration, development and exploitation; and companies operating national railways or urban railways invested by the State.[150] This means that the State will not divest from certain companies in the PetroVietnam, Electricity of Vietnam, Vietnam National Coal – Mineral Industries Holding Corporation Limited or Vietnam Post and Telecommunication groups.[151]
- **65% State Ownership** – The State will continue to own at least 65% of the charter capital of large-scale SOEs operating in, among other things, operating airports; large-scale mining; operating ports in special seaports; banking and finance and food wholesale that ensures major balances of the economy, stabilises the market and carries out political tasks.[152] These sectors include Agribank and Airports Corporation of Vietnam.[153]
- **50% State Ownership** – The State will continue to own half of the charter capital of SOEs in the following sectors, amongst others: water supply and drainage; basic chemicals; air transportation; large-scale companies in import/export of petroleum; cigarette manufacturing; and telecom infrastructure.[154] This means that the State technically can partially divest from companies such as Vinachem, Vinataba and Vietnam Airlines (although it is unlikely, at least in the near future).[155]
- There are some sectors where state ownership can fall from 50% or below, or full divestment is possible: manufacturing, real estate, agriculture, forestry, electricity production and retailing, telecommunications, and construction.

[149] *See* section 'Limits on Dispositions by the State' for further details.

[150] Section I of the Appendix to Decision 22/2021/QĐ-TTg of the Prime Minister dated 2 Jul. 2021 issuing a criteria and categorisation list of State-owned enterprises for ownership conversion, restructuring or divestment in the period 2021 – 2025 (***Decision 22***).

[151] Appendix I of Decision 1479/QĐ-TTg of the Prime Minister dated 29 Nov. 2022 approving the plan for restructuring of SOEs (***Decision 1479***).

[152] Section II of the Appendix to Decision 22.

[153] Appendix II of Decisions 1479.

[154] Section III of the Appendix to Decision 22.

[155] Appendix IV of Decisions 1479 states that the divestment plan in respect of those companies will be decided according to specific decisions of the Prime Minister.

4.2 Equitisation and State Divestment: Different Regulations

[154] There are two main avenues through which the State sells interests in its companies:

- In an equitisation process, an SOE is turned into a JSC and some (often not very many) of its shares are sold to employees and outsiders. In some cases, notably the equitisations of the State insurance company (Bao Viet), two of the State banks (Vietcombank and Vietinbank), one of the State beer companies (Habeco), one of the State airlines company (Vietnam Airlines), outsiders have included foreign strategic investors.
- The other process is through the State divesting interests in a company that has already been turned into a JSC. Notable divestment transactions have included the sale of a 54% interest in Saigon Beer Company (Sabeco) for about USD5 bn and the acquisition by Jardines of an interest in Vinamilk for about USD1 bn. As of early 2021, the Vietnamese Government is planning to divest its interest in some major listed companies such as FPT, Bao Viet Insurance, Bao Minh Insurance, VnSteel and Vinatex.

4.3 Equitisation: Different Principles for Strategic and Normal Investors

[155] Foreign investors wishing to acquire interests in SOEs undergoing equitisation have two main choices:

(1) buying shares as a strategic investor; and
(2) buying shares as a non-strategic investor in the initial offering of such shares to the public.

4.4 Equitisation: Strategic Investors

(a) Buying Shares as a Strategic Investor

[156] A selection of qualifying strategic investors will be made prior to the initial auction of shares to the public. If there is only one qualifying strategic investor,[156] the foreign strategic investor can buy the shares via a privately negotiated deal. A privately negotiated deal allows (at least in theory) a buyer to negotiate some

[156] This can be the case if the qualification criteria are drafted narrowly. For example, in the equitisation of PetroVietnam Oil Company (PV Oil), only those companies that had invested in refineries in Vietnam or committed to do so qualified. (Decision 1979 of the Prime Minister dated 8 Dec. 2017 ratifying the equitisation of PV Oil.).

minority protections. In addition, a foreign investor making an investment at this stage would have more certainty about the number of shares that it can purchase than if it purchased at the time of the auction to the public.

[157] The problem with privately negotiated purchases is that they are subject to a wide range of bureaucratic consents and uncertainty in the capital structure of the SOE. Foreigners are therefore rarely successful. And while domestic investors have a greater ability to navigate the difficulties, a consortium between a foreign investor and a domestic entity faces numerous challenges.

[158] In the context of SOEs for which there is investor competition, the main deterrents have been a combination of high prices and poor information (probably driven by a combination – in many State-owned entities – of poor information systems and the spectral presence of skeletons best left undisturbed). Unless investors are allowed to undertake meaningful due diligence or are willing to take strategic bets on the future of a company over which they have little influence (more common perhaps among Asian investors than Western ones), recent cases show that attempted auctions among strategic investors are unlikely to fare well. Unfortunately, strategic investors cannot 'wait out' the auction process and hope to reach a bilateral agreement during the equitisation. In recent cases, the Government has refused extensions. The potential investor, therefore, has to wait for a new process of State divestment of (unsold) shares to begin or for the equitised company (with State approval) to do a private placement of new equity.

(b) Strategic Investors

[159] Only companies in which the State retains more than a 50% interest can offer shares to strategic shareholders.[157]

[160] The selection of strategic investors that qualify to acquire a strategic stake in a company's equitisation has to be made prior to the initial offering of shares to the public (***IPO***).[158] In order to qualify to be a strategic investor, an investor must:

(i) have the financial capability, must have been profitable in the previous two years, and have no accumulated losses; and
(ii) provide written undertakings (x) to maintain the main business activities and brand names of the relevant SOEs for at least three years; (y) not to sell the shares it acquires for three years (two years less than the former regulations, though nothing precludes the equitising company from insisting on a longer lock-up as a contractual matter); and (z) to provide support to the equitised company in respect of the 'transfer of new technologies, human resources training, strengthening of financial capacity, corporate governance, supply of raw materials and materials, and/or development of a product consumption market'.[159]

---

157 Article 6.3(b) of Decree 126/2017/ND-CP of the Government dated 16 Nov. 2017 on conversion of 100% State-owned enterprises into JSCs, as amended on 30 Nov. 2020 (***Decree 126***). Please refer to section 'Limits on Dispositions by the State' for more details.

158 Article 6.3(c) of Decree 126.

159 Article 6.3(a) of Decree 126.

[161] The above criteria leave room for exact requirements to be set in the context of each specific equitisation. The government entity in charge of the equitisation[160] would decide the specific criteria based on the recommendation of the body responsible for implementing the equitisation, which is known as the Equitisation Steering Committee.[161]

(c) Price: Strategic Investor

[162] A strategic shareholder may purchase shares at either the agreed price (if there is only one potential strategic investor)[162] or at the successful auction price (if there is an auction among potential strategic shareholders),[163] provided that such price must not be lower than the average successful price in the IPO.[164]

[163] The strategic investor is required to put down a security deposit of 20% of the value of the shares for which it registers to subscribe at the starting price set out in the equitisation plan.[165] The investor loses the deposit if it fails to bid to buy such shares at a price set out in the preceding paragraph (which may not be known until the completion of the IPO).

(d) Ownership Percentage: Strategic Investor

[164] The maximum ownership interest that a strategic investor can acquire will be decided by the Equitisation Steering Committee (subject to approval by the competent authorities).

(e) Lock-Up Period: Strategic Investor

[165] The lock-up period for a strategic investor is at least three years.[166] This suggests that a longer lock-up period may be required by the Equitisation Steering Committee or by the company being equitised. Lock-ups of up to ten years have been demanded in practice, particularly in respect of businesses that are seen as having national security components. This was the case, for example, in the equitisation of PV Oil.[167] The argument on the Vietnamese side has often been linked to a fear of Chinese entities acquiring strategic interests in sensitive businesses. But as there are other means of protection against this concern, the argument has not fared well, and the authors are not aware of any lock-up of more than five years having been agreed.

[166] The lock-up period is sometimes inserted into the investment contract between the equitising SOE and the strategic investor on the basis that the law requires it. When this occurs, it adds a contractual overlay to a legal basis. If, for

[160] Depending on the State-owned enterprise being equitised, different government entities have the authority to make the decision approving its equitisation plan.

[161] Article 6.3(c) of Decree 126.

[162] Article 6.3(d) of Decree 126.

[163] *Ibid.*

[164] Article 6.3(d) and (đ) of Decree 126. *See* section 'Equitisation: Buying in the Initial Offering'.

[165] Article 6.3(h) of Decree 126. The starting price is theoretically the lowest acceptable share price based on the State's valuation of the company.

[166] Article 6.3(a) of Decree 126.

[167] Decision 1979 of the Prime Minister dated 8 Dec. 2017 ratifying the equitisation of PV Oil.

example, the law is subsequently changed to reduce or remove the lock-up (as recently occurred through Decree 126), any investor that has agreed contractually to a longer lock-up would still have to respect such undertaking.

(f) Currency of the Purchase

[167] The transaction must be carried out in Vietnamese Dong.[168] If the acquisition is large and expensive, and the investor is foreign, substantial planning with the foreign exchange desk of the investor's bank in Vietnam is advisable.

4.5 Equitisation: Buying in the Initial Offering

[168] An acquisition of shares during an IPO is the simplest means (though sadly, this is relative, and one cannot say that it is simple) by which foreign investors can acquire shares in an equitisation, as this involves no negotiations, approvals or lock-ups. Depending on the decision of the competent authority, an initial offering can be conducted by public auction, underwriting, direct negotiation and book-building.[169] Decree 126 for the first time provides for book-building. However, only the Prime Minister can decide which SOEs will be eligible to carry out book-building IPOs, and this method needs to follow the procedures set out in Circular 21/2019 of the MOF dated 11 April 2019.

[169] Investors buying shares in the IPO may not be able to buy as many shares as they would like. Depending on the capital structure of the SOE, there might be a limit imposed on the number of shares available to a single bidder.[170] There is always, of course, some uncertainty associated with buying shares on the open market.

4.6 State Divestment

(a) Forms of Divestments of State Capital

[170] The regulations[171] contain four means by which the State can divest itself of State capital:[172]

(i) Public auction sales: there are two types of public auctions: (x) normal public auctions with no limit on the number of shares that can be bought by a bidder,

---

[168] Article 7.1 of Decree 126.

[169] Article 7.2 of Decree 126.

[170] This tended to be more a problem when foreign investors were flocking to Vietnam. It is less likely to be an issue in the less frenetic environment that currently prevails.

[171] Article 4.5 of Decree 91/2015/ND-CP of the Government dated 13 Oct. 2015 on investment of State capital in enterprises and management and usage of capital and assets in enterprises (***Decree 91***), as amended by Decree 32/2018/ND-CP of the Government dated 8 Mar. 2018 (***Decree 32***), as amended by Decree 121/2020/ND-CP of the Government dated 9 Oct. 2020 and Decree 140/2020/ND-CP of the Government dated 30 Nov. 2020.

[172] Articles 1.13 and 1.16 of Decree 32.

and (y) public auctions for blocks, with the bidder having to buy all (but not some) shares of the offered block. Decree 32 requires that auctions of shares with a par value of VND10 bn or more have to be conducted on a stock exchange.

(ii) Competitive offerings: under Decree 32, there must be at least two bidders participating in a competitive offering. There is no clear distinction between a public auction sale and a competitive offering. Apparently, an auction sale must follow the statutory auction regulations and be conducted on the stock exchange (if the par value is VND10 bn or more), whereas a competitive offering can be conducted by the company or a securities company in accordance with the competitive offering regulations decided by the company itself.

(iii) Negotiated sales: a negotiated sale is a transfer of shares pursuant to a direct negotiation between the company and an investor.

(iv) Book-building: subject to approval from the Prime Minister, the sale of shares can be done by way of book-building.

[171] For a public company, the type of divestment that is possible is more limited than may appear from the above. The sale of a public company's shares off the stock exchange requires the State-owned company to first have tried to sell the shares via a public auction; failing this, the company must try to sell the shares via a competitive offering, and only then can it sell the shares via a negotiated sale.

(b) Price

[172] There are some limitations on the price for which the State capital can be sold:

(i) if the sale is conducted on the stock exchange, the selling price must be within the trading band of the exchange provided that it is not lower than the starting price (determined by an authorised valuer); and

(ii) if the sale is conducted by way of a public auction, a competitive offering or a negotiated sale, the selling price must not be lower than the reference trading price on the auction date, the date of the competitive offering or the date of signing the share purchase agreement (in case of a negotiated sale) provided that it is not lower than the starting price.

5 PUBLIC COMPANY ACQUISITIONS

5.1 General

[173] There are now thousands of public companies[173] in Vietnam.[174] Many transactions involve public companies. The Securities Law and relevant regulations,

[173] A 'public company' is defined under Art. 32.1 of the Securities Law as (i) a company that has a contributed charter capital of at least VND30 bn and at least 10% of whose voting shares are held by at least 100 investors who are not major shareholders; or (ii) a company that has successfully made an initial public offering. Companies that do not meet these conditions are still treated as public companies if they had been listed on the HOSE/HNX or registered for trading on the UPCom before the effective date of the Securities Law, i.e., on 1 Jan. 2021.

[174] *See* https://ssc.gov.vn/webcenter/portal/ubck/pages_r/m/csdlcngty.

in particular Decree 155, regulate the acquisition of shares of a public company in Vietnam, including through PTOs.

[174] The process of acquiring shares in a public company is not always the same. The main differences arise from:

(i) whether the acquisition requires a PTO;
(ii) whether the public company is listed on a stock exchange or registered for trading on the UPCom or not; and
(iii) whether the acquisition is part of a process of privatisation of a State-owned company.

5.2 Majority Transactions

[175] There have been few foreign acquisitions of the majority of a public company in Vietnam. This is because:

(a) the tender offer rules are not well developed;
(b) there is still a 49% foreign ownership cap for the majority of public companies (though this is slowly changing);
(c) where there is no foreign ownership cap, there is still a lack of clarity, difficulty and delay in taking a company private; and
(d) there are impediments to transacting at a price that is outside a specified trading band.

5.3 Hostile Transactions

[176] There is no distinction between a friendly and a hostile acquisition under Vietnamese law. Nearly all acquisitions in Vietnam are friendly, partly because substantial information relating to the target is often either not available or of suspect quality.

[177] There have been a few 'hostile' bids by domestic companies, such as Eximbank's attempt to take over Sacombank[175] and Masan's bid to take over Vietnam Coffee Corporation (***Vinacafe***). Generally, these have occurred through acquisitions by nominees of the hostile bidder of shares that are sufficient to call a meeting of

[175] In January 2012, Eximbank purchased 9.73% of the shares in Sacombank from ANZ following the approval of the SBV. Both Sacombank and Eximbank are local joint stock commercial banks that are listed on the HOSE. On 20 Feb. 2012, Eximbank publicly claimed that it had been 'authorised' by other shareholders of Sacombank (whose shares in aggregate, together with the shares held by Eximbank, represented more than 51% of the shares of Sacombank) to exercise the shareholder rights (including voting rights) of such other shareholders. Therefore, Eximbank claimed that it controlled more than 51% of the shares of Sacombank. On the same date, Eximbank sent a letter to Sacombank proposing to elect a new board of directors. Sacombank considered Eximbank's move as hostile and took certain defensive actions.

shareholders and call a vote to replace management.[176] Depending on the shares that are controlled, the bidder also strikes deals with significant minority shareholders. The legality of some of the manoeuvres using nominee shareholders is open to significant doubt. Foreign bidders in particular should be especially careful before using nominees.

5.4 Public Tender Offer (*PTO*)

(a) PTO Requirements

[178] A PTO is required for a person or group of related persons[177] to purchase shares (the 'buyer') in a public company in the following cases:[178]

(i) the buyer intends to purchase voting shares leading to ownership of 25% or more of the total voting shares of a public company;

(ii) a buyer holding 25% or more of the voting shares in a public company purchases additional voting shares, leading to its ownership of voting shares in that company reaching any of the 35%, 45%, 55%, 65% and 75% thresholds; and

---

176 In 2020, Kusto requested an extra-ordinary general meeting of shareholders to change the board and management of Conteccon (*see*, https://vir.com.vn/stakeholders-setting-precedent-over-control-of-coteccons-board-80293.html).

177 Related persons are defined in Art. 4.46 of the Securities Law to mean individuals and/or organisations with interactive relations in the following circumstances: (a) a company and its insiders; a public fund or public securities investment company and its insiders; (b) a company and any organisation or individual owing more than ten (10)% of the voting shares or capital contribution of such company; (c) an organisation or individual who in a relationship with another organisation or individual directly or indirectly controls or is jointly controlled by such other organisation or individual, or is subject to the same control with such other organisation or individual; (d) an individual and his/her biological parents, adoptive parents, parents-in-law, spouse, offspring, adopted children, daughter-in-law, son-in-law, siblings, brother-in-law or sister-in-law; (dd) a securities investment fund management company and securities investment funds or securities investment companies managed by such securities investment fund management company; (e) a contractual relationship in which one organisation or individual is the representative of the other; and (f) any other organisations and/or individuals being related persons as stipulated in the Enterprise Law.

Under Art. 4.23 of Enterprise Law, related parties of a company are individuals or organisations that have either a direct or an indirect relationship with such company in the following cases: (i) the parent company, managers or the legal representatives of the parent company or the persons competent to appoint/designate such managers are related persons of subsidiaries in the same group; (ii) subsidiaries, managers or legal representatives of such subsidiaries are related parties of the parent company in the same group; (iii) an individual, an organisation, a group of individuals or a group of organisations who have control over (x) the operation either through ownership, or shares acquisitions, in such company or (y) the decision making of such company; (iv) the company managers, the legal representative, the inspector of such company; (v) spouse, parents, adoptive parents, parents-in-law, children, adopted children, blood brothers, blood sisters, brothers-in-law, sisters-in-law of the enterprise manager or the legal representative of the inspector or the members/partners/shareholders who have the controlling stake or shares; (vi) any person authorised to represent one of the persons or companies mentioned in (i), (ii), (iii), (iv) and (v) above; or (vii) a company (***first company***) in which any person or company mentioned in (i), (ii), (iii), (iv), (v) or (vi) above having an ownership in the first company to the extent that they have control over the decision making of the first company.

178 Article 35.1 of the Securities Law.

(iii) a 'mandatory' bid discussed in paragraph (e) (Mandatory Bid) below.

[179] A public company may issue new shares to shareholders in a PTO.[179]

[180] A PTO requires registration with and approval from the SSC.

[181] There are certain exceptions to the need for a PTO, including:[180]

(i) the purchase of newly issued shares in accordance with an issuance plan approved by the general meeting of shareholders of the target company;
(ii) the purchase of secondary voting shares which has been approved by the general meeting of shareholders of the target company provided that such approval has identified the buyer;
(iii) the transfer of shares between companies within a parent-subsidiary; and
(iv) the purchase of shares in an auction or in a public offering, or of shares held by the State or by an SOE[181] in another company.

[182] Unlike the former Securities Law 2006, the MOF no longer has the discretion to exempt other PTOs.

[183] The concert party rules are vaguely drafted but in practice are believed to be loosely enforced (if at all) by the authorities. Indeed, there have been some indications that the concept of parties acting in concert is either not understood or ill-appreciated.

(b) Cross-Border Structures

[184] Although mergers are possible between Vietnamese companies, they are not possible for foreign companies in a cross-border transaction. Nor is it possible for a foreign buyer to set up a Vietnamese acquisition vehicle purely for the purposes of effecting a merger. The result is that most acquisitions of public companies occur by means of the purchase of shares of existing shareholders for cash.[182] This of course can lead to numerous issues, depending on the goals of the buyer. There are a few structuring alternatives that do not veer into unenforceable nominee arrangements.

(c) Board Actions

[185] Within ten days after receipt of the tender documents, the board of a target company has to send its opinions both to the SSC and to its shareholders. If there are any dissenting board members, their opinions have to be disclosed.[183]

---

[179] Article 53 of Decree 155.

[180] Article 35.2 of the Securities Law.

[181] SOEs are defined under Art. 4.11 of the Enterprise Law to include companies in which the State holds more than 50% of the charter capital or total voting shares.

[182] Although there is nothing which would prohibit Vietnamese shareholders from receiving shares in a foreign company as payment for the shares they held in the Vietnamese company, there would be various difficulties to overcome, including obtaining the SBV's approval for such foreign share ownership. The SBV could, but would not have to, take the view that such ownership was permissible on the basis that no money has left the country.

[183] Article 87 of Decree 155.

[186] A target company can take various steps to frustrate an acquisition, though it should be noted that hostile bids are almost non-existent at the current time. For example, it can:

(i) increase or reduce the volume of voting shares through a split or consolidation or conversion of preferred shares;
(ii) reduce its equity capital;
(iii) issue additional securities to increase its charter capital; or
(iv) sell the whole or a material (35% or more) part of its assets.

[187] In each of the above situations, the offeror can withdraw its tender.[184]

(d) Partial Offers

[188] Partial offers are contemplated by the law. The aggregate foreign ownership in a public company is potentially limited. The buyer's tender offer may therefore be for a number of shares that is smaller than those offered for sale. In such a case, it must buy shares in proportion to the shares registered for sale by each shareholder. The buyer has to pay the same price to all shareholders.[185]

[189] A buyer can withdraw their offer if the minimum specified number of shares is not tendered.[186]

[190] The exact mechanics of partial offers should be discussed with the SSC.

[191] A buyer might be able to buy the shares of enough small shareholders to take a company to the point where it is no longer public. Under Decree 155, a public company is required to notify the SSC within fifteen days after the date on which it does not satisfy the conditions to be considered a public company.[187] But it can only be deregistered as a public company one year after the date on which the company fails to satisfy such conditions.[188] There are some limited exceptions to the one-year rule, which arise when the public company is consolidated, merged, becomes bankrupt, dissolved, converted into another form or owned by another person.[189] These exceptions aside, the one-year rule suggests that a public company cannot easily and quickly be restructured by way of reducing the number of shareholders to less than 100 in order to avoid the restrictions applicable to public companies.

(e) Mandatory Bids

[192] Except where a PTO is for all shares with voting rights, the law requires that if, at the end of a tender offer tranche, the offeror holds 80% or more of the shares of a public company, then the offeror must continue to offer to purchase the

---

184 Article 92.1 of Decree 155.

185 Article 93.5 of Decree 155.

186 Article 92.1(a) of Decree 155.

187 Article 38.1 of the Securities Law.

188 Article 38.2 of the Securities Law.

189 Article 8 of Circular 118/2020/TT-BTC of the MOF dated 31 Dec. 2020 providing guidance on offering, issuing of shares, public tendering, redemption of shares, registration and de-registration of public companies.

remaining voting shares for the next thirty days at the same price and on the same payment terms as the first tender offer.[190]

[193] The offeror must notify the SSC of the continued tender offer within five days after the final date for shareholders to accept the tender offer under the first PTO.[191]

(f) Buying Shares Outside a Bid

[194] During the period from the corporate approval of the tender offer (applicable to a corporate buyer) or from the submission of the PTO dossier to the SSC (applicable to an individual buyer) until the completion of the purchase, the bidder is not permitted to directly or indirectly purchase or undertake to purchase shares outside the PTO.[192]

(g) Terms of a PTO

(i) Consideration

[195] The offer price must not be less than:[193]

(A) the average of (x) if the shares are listed, the reference price announced on the stock exchange or (y) if the shares are unlisted, the reference price quoted by two securities companies, for the period of sixty consecutive days preceding the date of submission of the PTO dossier to the SSC (the 'sixty-day period'); and

(B) the highest purchase price in the PTO during the sixty-day period.

(ii) Equality of Offer

[196] If a buyer makes a PTO, such an offer must be available equally to all shareholders of the target company.[194] The offeror has to provide complete information to all shareholders of the target company at the same time so as to enable them to be in the same position to assess the proposal.[195]

(iii) Other Classes

[197] There are no legal obligations on the buyer to purchase all classes of securities of the target company.

(iv) Financing Condition

[198] The offeror has to submit to the SSC, as part of the application for registration of the PTO, a bank guarantee or a confirmation of a blocked bank account with sufficient funds to ensure its financial capability to implement the offer.[196]

---

[190] Article 35.1(c) of the Securities Law.

[191] Article 94 of Decree 155. *See* section 'Squeeze-outs'.

[192] Article 89.1(a) of Decree 155.

[193] Article 91 of Decree 155.

[194] Article 89.1(c) of Decree 155.

[195] Article 89.1(d) of Decree 155.

[196] Article 85.1(d) of Decree 155.

(h) Timetable

[199] A PTO must remain open for at least thirty days and no longer than sixty days.[197] Shareholders of the target company who have accepted a tender offer may withdraw their acceptance if the tender conditions change or a competitive tender is made.[198] Competitive tenders have not yet occurred in Vietnam.

(i) Tender Documents

[200] A PTO must be registered with the SSC. The file for registration must include the following:[199]

(i) a public tender registration, in the form stipulated by the MOF;
(ii) information disclosure, in the form stipulated by the MOF;
(iii) the decision of the board approving the public tender;
(iv) the bank guarantee or confirmation on blocking of the bank account verifying the financial capability of the bidder;
(v) a document issued by the securities company acting as the PTO agent confirming the agency status; and
(vi) a merger clearance issued by the VCC (where applicable under the Competition Law) (*see* section 'Merger Control').

[201] The SSC has fifteen days from receiving a complete and valid dossier to confirm or reject the PTO registration.[200]

(j) Publicity

[202] Bidders are normally careful about publicity. During the offer, the law prohibits a bidder from providing different levels of information to different shareholders or providing information to them at different times.[201] The prohibition is stated in general terms.

(k) Withdrawal of Bids

[203] A bidder can withdraw its bid if the number of shares accepting the tender offer is less than the minimum number for which the tender was registered. It can also be withdrawn if the target company:[202]

(i) increases or reduces the volume of voting shares through a split or consolidation or conversion of preferred shares;
(ii) reduces its equity capital;
(iii) issues additional securities to increase its charter capital; or
(iv) sells the whole or a material (35% or more) part of its assets.

[197] Article 93.2 of Decree 155.
[198] Article 93.4 of Decree 155.
[199] Article 85 of Decree 155.
[200] Article 86.3 of Decree 155.
[201] Article 89.1(d) of Decree 155.
[202] Article 92.1 of Decree 155.

(l) Announcements and Disclosure Obligations

(i) There is no legal requirement that information relating to negotiations be made public.

(ii) The bidder has to send the relevant data for the application for registration of a tender to the SSC and to the target company. The target company has to disclose information relating to a PTO on its website and the relevant Vietnamese stock exchange within three days from the date of receipt of the application.[203]

(iii) The offeror is required to announce a PTO publicly on the websites of the offeror (if any), the PTO agent and the relevant Vietnamese stock exchange within seven days after receipt of the SSC's registration of the tender offer.[204] The PTO can only be implemented after (A) the SSC has confirmed receipt of a complete PTO registration dossier, and (B) three days have elapsed after the public announcement by the offeror.

(iv) If there is a merger involving a public company, the relevant resolution of the general meeting of shareholders approving such merger must be disclosed on its website (and, in the case of a listed company on the relevant Vietnamese stock exchange) within twenty four hours of being passed.

(m) Squeeze-outs

[204] The tender offer rules do not have any 'squeeze out' rights, enabling the offeror to purchase shares from the remaining shareholders without the consent of such shareholders after the offeror purchases a certain percentage of shares. However, an offeror has to 'continue to purchase the remaining shares' for thirty days from the time it becomes the holder of 80% or more of the shares in a target company.[205] There is no obligation on the remaining shareholders to sell during such a thirty-day period.[206]

(n) Sanctions

[205] Failure to comply with the takeover rules could result in administrative penalties.[207] In addition, an acquisition that is not conducted through a tender process in contravention of the law could be challenged. Furthermore, violating parties risk claims or enforcement proceedings brought by the SSC or minority shareholders.

---

[203] Article 86.2 of Decree 155.

[204] Article 93.1(a) of Decree 155.

[205] Article 94 of Decree 155.

[206] Under the Enterprise Law, a shareholder voting against such a resolution may demand that the company redeem its shares. A shareholder with 65% or more of the shares (or a higher percentage if so provided in the charter) of a company may indirectly 'force' the remaining shareholders to redeem their shares, by, for example, the majority shareholder passing a resolution to reorganise the company (for example, merger, split or conversion) or to change the shareholder rights recorded in the charter of the company.

[207] The administrative penalties would depend on the specific breach and could be up to VND1 500 m (approximately USD63 830). Failure to register a public tender with the SSC could result in a fine of VND200 m (approximately USD8 511) to VND300 m (approximately USD12 766). Article 17 of Decree 156/2020/ND-CP of the Government dated 31 Dec. 2020 providing regulations on dealing with administrative breaches in securities sectors and securities market.

5.5 Transaction Process

(a) Acquisition of Listed Shares on the Exchange

[206] Shares in Vietnam are listed on either of the two exchanges (i.e., the HOSE or the HNX)[208] or registered for trading on the UPCom market (the over-the-counter market at the HNX). In order to list securities on the HOSE or the HNX or to register securities for trading on the UPCom market, an issuer must meet certain requirements and apply to the relevant exchange.[209]

[207] Listed shares can be traded by means of either order matching or by a put-through trade. Trades on the exchange must occur within a certain range[210] of the reference price on the trading day immediately preceding the date of sale unless the parties obtain special approval to trade outside the band from the SSC.

[208] Even if the sales price is within the band when the share sale agreement is signed, there is a risk that the price will move outside the band during the period between signing and completion of the transaction. There are various possible ways of dealing with the issue, such as price adjustment mechanisms and offshore equalisations, but all of them face difficulties. The usual practice in a transaction involving shares in listed companies has been to obtain approval to trade off the exchange from the SSC.[211]

(b) Acquisition of Listed Shares off the Exchange

[209] Except in limited circumstances,[212] listed shares must be traded on the exchange. The SSC may approve an off-exchange transaction on a case-by-case based on some or all of the following documents:[213]

---

208 From 1 July 2023, the HNX stopped receiving applications for listing on HNX. From 1 Jul. 2023 to 31 Dec. 2023 and from 1 Jan. 2025 to 31 Jun. 2025, the HNX will transfer all the companies listed on HNX to the HOSE. Circular 57/2021/TT-BTC of the MOF dated 12 Jul. 2021 on restructuring of stock market.

209 https://ssc.gov.vn/webcenter/portal/ubck/pages_r/m/thngtinthtrng/thngkthtrng.

210 The trading band currently is +/-10% on the HNX, +/-7% on the HOSE and +/-15% on the UPCom.

211 As a matter of practice at the time of writing this article, the SSC is reluctant to issue such special approval.

212 These include (i) donation or inheritance of securities; (ii) redemption of shares from employees under an ESOP; (iii) redemption of shares from employees and officers who acquired shares under a preferential offering in accordance with the equitisation regulations; (iv) redemption of shares at the shareholder's request or from shareholders pro rata to their shareholding; (v) transfers of shares by a founding shareholder during the lock-up period; (vi) transfers of shares from an entrusting investor to the entrusted fund management company and vice versa or between entrusted fund management companies at the request of the entrusting investor; (vii) transfers pursuant to a court judgement, an arbitral award or a decision of an enforcement agency; (viii) demerger, merger, consolidation or capital contribution by shares; (ix) transfers pursuant to a public tender offer; (x) transfers of State capital or capital held by SOEs in other companies under an auction, competitive tendering or book-build; (xi) public offering by shareholders of public companies pursuant to an auction on a stock exchange; (xii) transfers pursuant to borrowing or lending of securities; (xiii) transfers of shares for the purposes of issuing or cancelling depository certificates between investors and an offshore depository certificate issuer; (xiv) transfers of ownership resulting from enforcement of security; (xv) transfers of preference shares which are not subject to restrictions on transfer; (xvi) transfers of base shares for the exercise of covered warrants; (xvii) transfers of shares between foreign

(i) a letter requesting for trading off the exchange;
(ii) copy of the share purchase agreement;
(iii) corporate approvals of the transfer (applicable to local parties);
(iv) if applicable, approval by the shareholders of the target company approving that the transfer can be done without a PTO;
(v) letter issued by the target company confirming that it is aware of the transaction and does not object to it;
(vi) confirmation by the depository member (if applicable) or the target company on the number of transferring shares held by the transferor(s);
(vii) letter from the regulatory authority in a regulated sector on the transfer of the shares in the target company;
(viii) copies of business or incorporation certificate/licences of each of the purchaser and seller (if institutional) or ID cards (if individual);
(ix) copies of securities trading codes of the purchaser and the seller;
(x) evidence of authority of the signatories to the transaction agreement; and
(xi) letter from the purchaser and the seller explaining matters as may be requested by the SSC, such as disclosure of information, non-cash payment, and sources of funding for the payment.

[210] The SSC will have seven business days to review an application dossier for the trading of the exchange to request additional information. It then will have to either approve or disapprove within ten days of receiving a complete dossier.[214]

[211] Like most other approvals in Vietnam, the SSC's approval is discretionary. The SSC may refuse to give the approval if it is not provided with all the documents set out above. It may also refuse if it has a reason to suspect that the transaction is not in line with the law. That said, we are not aware of a transaction where parties supported by good brokers have not managed to obtain the SSC's approval.

[212] After obtaining the approval from the SSC, the parties apply to the VSD for the transfer of shares directly at the VSD.

[213] Despite the general timeline to process an application for off-exchange trading discussed above, it is difficult to estimate how much time is needed to accomplish all the relevant steps in practice.[215]

(c) Acquisitions of Unlisted Public Companies

[214] At law, promptly after becoming a public company, the company should register as such with the SSC. After doing so,[216] it would also have to register its shares

investors where the foreign ownership cap was met, at a negotiated price which is higher than the ceiling price of the shares at the time of trading; and (xviii) other cases as decided by the SSC. Article 6.2 of Circular 119/2020/TT-BTC of the MOF dated 31 Dec. 2020 providing guidelines on registration, depository, clearing and settlement of securities transactions (***Circular 119***).

213 Article 6.3 of Circular 119.

214 Article 6.4 of Circular 119.

215 *See* footnote 227.

216 Under the regulations this has to occur within ninety days after a company meets the conditions for being a public company, but there is nothing to prevent it from occurring sooner.

with the VSD. Once registered, such shares should be deposited at the VSD through the local broker (or custodian bank).

[215] Any transfer of shares of an unlisted public company to a buyer should be implemented through the VSD, and the transfer would become effective when the VSD records the transfer.[217]

[216] At law, all public companies must register and deposit their shares at the VSD and register for trading on the UPCom (if it is not listed on a stock exchange).[218] In practice, not all public companies have registered and deposited their shares at the VSD or registered for trading on the UPCom. It appears that there have been various examples of transfers of public company shares without that company having registered its shares with the VSD and/or registered for trading on the UPCom. Investors in these cases seem to accept the risk based on the fact that their names and details will be recorded in the shareholder's register of the company.

[217] The risk for a buyer in following the practice rather than the regulations is that its title to the shares could be challenged on the basis that the shares were not transferred through the VSD, as required by law, and that it was not recorded at the VSD as the owner of the shares. In addition, the procedure for transferring shares in a public company is different from that applicable to a non-public company (e.g., a foreign buyer would be required to obtain an acquisition approval if it invests in a non-public company – *see* section 10.2 'Regulatory Approvals'). If a buyer agrees to buy shares in a public company that are not registered or deposited with VSD or registered for trading on the UPCom, it will insist the transaction be carried out according to the procedures applicable to non-public companies.

5.6 Securities Trading Code and Securities Trading Account

[218] Prior to purchasing shares in a public company in Vietnam, a foreign investor will have to obtain a securities trading code from the VSD.[219] Once the foreign investor has obtained its unique securities trading code, it may open a securities trading account, a securities depository account and accounts at a commercial bank in Vietnam,[220] each of which is linked to the securities trading code. A purchase or sale of listed shares by a foreign investor may only be carried out through these accounts. The securities trading account has to be opened with a local broker. The securities depository account may be opened at either the local broker or at a cus-

[217] *See* Decision 56/QD-UBCK of the MOF dated 31 Jan. 2013 on transfer of ownership of unlisted shares of public companies which have been registered with the VSD but not a stock exchange.

[218] Articles 48, 61 and 62 of the Securities Law.

[219] Article 138.2 of Decree 155. The procedure to obtain a securities trading code is straightforward but bureaucratic.

[220] Article 2.5 of Circular 51/2021/TT-BTC of the MOF dated 30 Jun. 2021 providing guidelines for obligations of individuals and organisations in foreign investment activities in the Vietnam stock market. Such commercial bank or foreign bank branch may be the custodian bank as well.

todian bank if the foreign investor appoints one.[221] If the foreign investor opens a securities depository account with a custodian bank, it must place its trading order with the local broker and make the settlement through the custodian bank.

5.7 Disclosure Obligations

(a) Reporting Requirement for 'Major Shareholders'

[219] A 'major shareholder'[222] (including its related persons) must file a report to the target, the SSC and the stock exchange within five days after becoming or ceasing to be a major shareholder.[223] The report includes details of the legal owner and its related persons (if the related persons are also shareholders of the company).

[220] When there is a change in shareholding ownership of a major shareholder in excess of +/- one per cent (1%) of the total voting shares of the company, for example, when a shareholder crosses the threshold of 6%, 7% or 8%, the 'major shareholder' must file a report to the company, the SSC and stock exchange (if the company is listed) within five days after each change.[224]

[221] The above disclosure obligations also apply to a group of related foreign shareholders holding 5% or more of the voting shares in a public company.[225]

[222] If the filing covers related shareholders, the report will be filed by the shareholder who enters into the share transaction, resulting in the relevant change.[226]

(b) Reporting Requirements for 'Internal Shareholders'

[223] An 'internal shareholder' or his/her related party must file a report (in the prescribed form) to the company, the SSC and the stock exchange at least three working days (but not more than thirty days) before the date of any transaction if the estimated par value of shares to be traded is VND50 m in a day or VND200 m in aggregate in a month.[227] The transaction can only be executed twenty-four

---

221 Branches in Vietnam of HSBC, Citibank and Deutsche Bank are licensed and approved as depository members and are commonly used as custodians by major foreign institutional investors (*see*, https://www.ssc.gov.vn/webcenter/portal/ubck/pages_r/m/csdlcngty/ngnhngluk).

222 'Major shareholders' are defined by the Securities Law as 'shareholders holding more than 5% of the voting shares in an issuer'.

223 Article 31.1 of Circular 96/2020/TT-BTC of the MOF dated 16 Nov. 2020 on public disclosure (***Circular 96***).

224 Article 31.2 of Circular 96.

225 Article 31.4 of Circular 96.

226 Article 31.5 of Circular 96.

227 'Internal shareholders' are defined as shareholders 'holding key positions in the management or executive bodies of the company'. Such 'key positions' include the chairman of the board, board members, legal representatives, the (general) director (i.e., chief executive officer), deputy (general) director (i.e., deputy chief executive officer), chief financial officer, chief accountant, and equivalent executive position appointed by the shareholders or the board or the chairman; the chief inspector and members of the inspection committee; members of the internal audit of the company; and person(s) authorised to make disclosures on behalf of the company. Article 4.45 of the Securities Law.

hours or more after the stock exchange has published such information. In the report, the shareholder does not disclose the price or the prospective buyer.[228]

[224] Five working days after completing the transaction, the 'internal shareholder' or his/her related person must report to the SSC, the stock exchange and the target company on the results of the transaction.[229]

5.8 Target Company Commitments

[225] Vietnamese law does not regulate break fees or exclusivity. These can be included in the purchase agreement, though without great certainty as to enforcement because the law does not specifically contemplate them. In practice, break fees are rare.

5.9 Due Diligence

[226] Neither the seller nor the target company is obliged to disclose any due diligence information to a buyer. The disclosure process, therefore, depends on what is agreed between the parties.

[227] Publicly available information is generally limited.[230] The buyer may obtain general registration information relating to the target company from the national system of information on enterprise registration. The buyer may also obtain information that is made publicly available by a public target company, including:

(a) information that is disclosed on a periodic basis (e.g., the audited annual financial statements, annual report, report on corporate governance and resolutions of shareholders' meetings);
(b) information that is disclosed on an extraordinary basis (such as information relating to the freezing of accounts, temporary suspension of part or all of the business, revocation of the business registration certificate and redemption of shares); and
(c) information disclosed at the request of the SSC or stock exchange (such as an event that seriously affects the lawful interests of investors and information relating to a public company that seriously affects the price of its shares).

[228] There are no explicit limitations on the target company's ability to provide information. However, receipt of non-public information could result in insider trading issues as an investor cannot purchase shares of a listed company based on information that is 'related to' that company, is not in the public domain and could

[228] Article 33.1 and Schedule XIII of Circular 96.
[229] Article 33.1(dd) of Circular 96.
[230] *See* section 'Due Diligence: Publicly Available Information'.

have a major impact on the price of shares of that company. There is no further legal detail about what this means in any particular situation.[231]

6 MERGERS

6.1 Overview

[229] Mergers of Vietnamese companies are still rare. The definition of a 'merger' is contained in Article 89 of the Civil Code and Article 201 of the Enterprise Law. These state that 'a legal entity may be merged into another legal entity pursuant to a decision of a competent State body or as agreed by such legal entities' and 'after a merger, the merged legal entity shall be wound up and the civil rights and obligations of such legal entity shall be transferred to the merging legal entity'. Article 88 of the Civil Code provides for the consolidation of two existing legal entities into a newly formed legal entity.

[230] The same foreign ownership limitations apply to a merger as to an acquisition if it involves a restricted sector. Similarly, mergers in sectors that are regulated by special laws may require special approvals. For example, a bank merger requires the approval of the SBV.[232]

6.2 Procedures

[231] The procedures for a merger under the Enterprise Law are as follows:

(a) The parties will need to prepare a merger contract (***Merger Contract***) and charter for the surviving company.[233] Although there have been few mergers in Vietnam, the Merger Contract appears to be the operative document whose registration will give legal effect to the various matters covered in it.
(b) The Merger Contract should contain all the details necessary to ensure that all rights, assets, privileges, obligations, liabilities and duties are transferred from the merging companies to the new or surviving company. The Enterprise Law suggests that this document should cover the following areas, though the list is not exhaustive:

---

[231] *See* discussion in section 'Due Diligence Issues' for general due diligence issues which may also be relevant to public company acquisitions and discussion in section 'Due Diligence of a Public Company and Insider Trading Rules' for more detail about insider trading.

[232] Circular 04/2010/TT-NHNN dated 11 Feb. 2010 of the SBV on acquisition, merger and consolidation of credit institutions (as amended by Circular 36/2015/TT-NHNN of the SBV dated 31 Dec. 2015 on restructuring of credit institutions). There were a number of domestic bank mergers between 2012 and 2015 as part of a Government restructuring plan for the banking sector. The SBV is also proposing to ask Vietcombank, MB Bank, VPBank, HDBank to acquire failed banks, including Construction Bank, OceanBank, GP Bank and DongA Bank as a part of the restructuring of the banking sector.

[233] Article 201.2 of the Enterprise Law.

(i) the procedures for and conditions of the merger;
(ii) an employment plan;
(iii) procedures, timings and conditions for transferring assets;[234]
(iv) procedures, timings and conditions for transferring capital contributions, shares and bonds; and
(v) the period for implementing the merger.

(c) Companies participating in a merger must comply with the merger filing requirements in the Competition Law.
(d) In addition, due to the lack of specific regulations on how mergers work as a matter of law, it would be prudent for the Merger Contract to cover: (i) all areas usually covered in other jurisdictions; (ii) all important rights, assets, privileges, obligations, liabilities and duties of the merged and surviving companies; and (iii) any issues special to Vietnam, such as the province where taxes will be paid.
(e) The charter should reflect the new organisation of the merging company.
(f) The members, owners or shareholders of the merging companies will need to approve the Merger Contract and the charter of the merging company and obtain a new enterprise registration certificate and/or an amended investment registration certificate of the surviving company in a merger (if applicable).
(g) One problem that can arise in practice is how to handle the merger of two companies that are licensed by different authorities, such as the DPI of Hanoi and the DPI of Ho Chi Minh City. Theoretically, the DPI responsible for the surviving company would inform the DPI for the disappearing company to update the national registration database after the merger to reflect the disappearing company's merger. In practice, the process is not so smooth.
(h) The Merger Contract will need to be sent to all creditors and notified to employees within fifteen days from the date of its approval.[235]

6.3 Implementation of Mergers

[232] The Enterprise Law refers to the 'conversion of the capital contribution, shares and bonds of the merged companies into the capital contribution, shares and bonds of the merging company' without stating how the conversion occurs. As few mergers have been implemented, and as the generality of the law provides little assistance, numerous issues have to be solved on an ad hoc basis. These include the following:

(a) Valuation of the relevant companies and the relationship between their shares for conversion purposes.
(b) If one of the companies is listed, it would be subject to the management of the SSC. The SSC may reach different conclusions about the merger from

[234] Vietnamese law does not contain guidance on how to exclude assets or liabilities from a merger.
[235] Article 201.2(b) of the Enterprise Law.

those reached by the DPI in the province where the relevant company is established.

(c) The tax rates applicable to the surviving company if the merged companies were subject to different profits tax rates and whether a new, more preferential tax rate might be applicable to the new enterprise because, for example, it is larger.

(d) The tax holidays available to the surviving company, provided the merged companies have used different amounts of the tax holidays initially granted to them.

(e) The ability to carry forward tax losses which may have built up in one of the merged companies.

(f) The applicability of investment rights or incentives available to new companies at the time of the merger if such investment rights or incentives were not available at the time the merged companies were originally licensed.

(g) How to ensure that the surviving company's rights over the disappearing company's land, and the land rental rates applicable to it, are specifically recorded in the land documents and the amended investment registration certificate issued upon the merger.

(h) How to record a disappearing company's branches – these would become branches of the surviving company upon the merger, and the surviving company would have to try to record them in the amended enterprise registration certificate issued to it upon the merger.

(i) How to make payment upon a cash-out merger – there are few precedents in Vietnam, so all payment issues would need to be addressed in the merger contract (the disappearing company's shareholders would presumably need to be comfortable that the structure would not result in a greater tax burden on them than if they had sold shares into the market).

(j) The effective date of the merger, which would normally be the date stipulated in the enterprise registration certificate or investment registration certificate issued upon the merger by the competent State authority.

(k) In a consolidation, all assets of the consolidating companies are inherited by the new company pursuant to the plan of consolidation. However, it is not clear whether this would absolve the new company from the need to obtain a new land use right certificate. In a merger, the same issue will arise in respect of the property of the disappearing company.

[233] Until greater clarity is visible in the law, or at least in practice, merging or consolidating companies should develop a full understanding of the rights and privileges that could be gained or lost through merger or consolidation. They should also analyse the possible negotiating leverage that could be gained through using a merger rather than a consolidation or vice versa. They should then present to the competent State authority, in their restructuring plan, the most desirable solution. At the current time, parties should be prepared for lengthy discussions in order to obtain official approval of their plan.

7 INVESTMENT INCENTIVES AND PROTECTIONS

7.1 General

[234] An investor in certain sectors or in certain specific locations in Vietnam may be entitled to various tax, accounting and land incentives.[236] The law is highly prescriptive regarding the sectors and areas that have investment incentives, though a catch-all clause allows appropriate projects to negotiate incentives even if they are not otherwise on the list. The investor should work directly with the relevant authority (whether tax, finance, customs or otherwise) to obtain incentives.[237]

7.2 Encouraged Investment Sectors

[235] Investments in the following sectors are entitled to certain incentives:[238]

(a) High-tech activities and industrial products which support them; research and development activities; and products applying scientific and technological research.
(b) Production of new materials, new energy, clean energy or renewable energy; production of products with an added value of 30% or more; and energy-saving products.
(c) Production of electronics, prioritised mechanical products, agricultural machinery, automobiles, automobile parts, and shipbuilding.
(d) Production of products in support industries in accordance with a priority list to be promulgated by the Government.[239]
(e) Production of information technology, software and digital content products.
(f) Breeding, growing and processing agricultural, forestry and aquaculture products; afforestation and protection of forests; salt production; fishing and fishing logistics; creation of plant and animal varieties and biological technology products.
(g) Collection, processing, reprocessing or reuse of refuse.
(h) Development, operation and management of infrastructure facilities; and development of public transportation in urban areas.
(i) Preschool education, general education, vocational education, and university education.
(j) Medical consultation and treatment; production of medicines, raw materials for production of medicines; storage of medicines; scientific research in relation to the production of new medicines; production of medical equipment and supplies.
(k) Investment in certain sports facilities; and protection and promotion of the value of cultural heritage.

---

[236] *See* generally Art. 15 of the Investment Law.
[237] Article 17 of the Investment Law.
[238] Article 16.1 of the Investment Law.
[239] Support industries are, in broad terms, those that support national industrial goals.

(l) Investment in centres for geriatrics, psychiatry or treatment of patients exposed to Agent Orange, and centres for the care of the elderly, disabled, orphans or street children without support.
(m) People's credit funds and micro-finance institutions.
(n) Production of goods or supply of services that create or participate in a value chain or an industry linkage cluster.

7.3 Encouraged Geographical Areas

[236] Investors are also entitled to incentives if they invest in:

(a) geographical locations whose socio-economic conditions are categorised as either difficult or especially difficult;[240] and
(b) industrial zones, export-processing zones, high technology zones and economic zones.[241]

7.4 Standard Investment Incentives: Tax

[237]

(a) Companies with projects in encouraged investment sectors and encouraged geographical areas are entitled to preferential tax rates for a specified number of years. Two preferential rates of 10% and 20% are available for fifteen years and ten years, respectively, starting from the commencement of operating activities.[242] As of 1 January 2016, enterprises entitled to the preferential CIT rate of 20% will be taxed at 17% instead.[243] When the right to a preferential rate expires, the standard rate becomes effective. Certain sectors that are oriented towards the public good, such as education and health, are entitled to a 10% rate for the life of the project.[244]
(b) Taxpayers may be eligible for a complete exemption from CIT for a specified number of years beginning immediately after the company first makes a profit, followed by a period where tax is charged at 50% of the applicable rate.[245] However, if a company has not made a profit for three years after the commencement of operations, the tax holiday/tax reduction will start from the fourth year of operations.[246]

240 Article 16.2 of the Investment Law and Annex III of Decree 31.

241 Article 16.2 of the Investment Law.

242 Article 13 of the Law on Corporate Income Tax of the National Assembly dated 3 Jun. 2008 (as amended on 1 Jan. 2014 and 1 Jan. 2015) (the ***CIT Law***).

243 Article 13 of the CIT Law.

244 Article 13.2 of the CIT Law.

245 Article 14.3 of the CIT Law.

246 *Ibid.*

(c) Additional tax reductions may be available for companies in manufacturing, construction and transportation activities that employ large numbers of female staff, or which employ ethnic minorities.[247]

(d) Foreign investors are also exempt from payment of import duty on equipment, materials, means of transportation and other goods for the implementation of their investment projects in Vietnam.

7.5 Standard Investment Incentives: Land

[238]

(a) The maximum term for a grant of land use rights for an investment project is normally fifty years. On rare occasions, this can be extended to seventy years for projects requiring large investments, whose rate of capital recovery is likely to be slow, and for projects in areas with difficult socio-economic conditions.[248]

(b) Investors in certain preferred investment sectors and geographical areas are entitled to exemption from or reduction of land rent, land use fees and land use tax in accordance with the laws on land and the laws on tax.[249] For example, investors in BOT projects are entitled to exemption or reduction from land payments.[250] The exemption from land payments, if applicable, has some unintended consequences though, because land can only be mortgaged if it has been fully paid, and the official position so far is that land that is exempted from payment has not been paid and so cannot be mortgaged. This poses financing hurdles for large-scale infrastructure projects and will affect potential buyers wishing to acquire such projects using debt.

(c) There are also some incentives for investors in industrial zones, export-processing zones, high-tech zones and economic zones, innovative start-ups and R&D activities.[251]

7.6 Special Investment Incentives

[239]

(a) Incentives higher than the standard ones may be granted by the Government for the following projects with significant socio-economic impact:[252]

---

247 Articles 15.1 and 15.2 of the CIT Law.

248 Article 126.3 of the Land Law.

249 Article 15 of the Investment Law.

250 Article 54.2 of Decree 43/2014/ND-CP of the Government dated 15 May 2014 (as amended on 3 Mar. 2017; 8 Feb. 2021 and 20 May 2023) providing implementation of the Land Law.

251 Articles 15 and 16 of the Investment Law.

252 Article 20 of the Investment Law; Decision 29/2021/QD-TTg of the Prime Minister dated 6 Oct. 2021 on regulations on special investment incentives.

(i) investment projects to develop or expand research and development (R&D) centres and creative innovation centres with a total investment capital of VND3 000 bn or more and disbursing at least VND1 000 bn within three years of issuance of the investment registration certificate or investment policy approval, and national creative innovation centres established pursuant to a decision of the Prime Minister;

(ii) investment projects in special preferential investment industries with investment capital of VND30 000 bn or more, disbursing at least VND10 000 bn within three years of issuance of the investment registration certificate or investment policy approval.

(b) Where encouragement of the development of something unusual is required, such as a special economic zone, or a very important and expensive project, such as the new Long Thanh international airport near Ho Chi Minh City, the Government may ask the National Assembly to issue investment incentives other than those stipulated in the Investment Law.[253]

7.7 Documentation of Investment Incentives

[240]

(a) Investment incentives should be recorded in the investment policy approval, investment registration certificate or project documents of all foreign projects that require them.[254] If incentives purport to exist that are not so recorded, buyers should be wary about them because they could be changed or eliminated without recourse. For this reason, buyers may insist that the target obtains the investment registration certificate to record the relevant investment incentives, even though the target is not required to obtain an investment registration certificate (e.g., because it is structured as a domestic investor).[255]

(b) In the past, certain important projects, usually in the infrastructure or heavy industry areas, were supported by Government guarantees. These guarantees, although extremely rare in practice,[256] covered numerous items, ranging from support for foreign exchange needs, to guarantees of performance by State-owned corporations that are essential to the project, to subsidies and to the nature of the competition that will be allowed to the project. The law no longer confers on the Prime Minister the right to provide such guarantees.[257] Thus,

253 Article 20.6 of the Investment Law.

254 Article 17 of the Investment Law.

255 Article 37.2 and 37.3 of the Investment Law.

256 Outside of the BOT context, where such guarantees were also rare, the only foreign investors that have received such guarantees have been in nationally important oil and gas projects, usually gas-to-power projects or oil refineries.

257 The revenue deficit sharing mechanism set out in Art. 82 of the PPP Law gives some predictability to PPP projects in terms of revenue, but normally this relates to operational deficits not non-payment by an offtaker. This would not apply to non-PPP projects.

any incentives desired by developers should be contained in the investment policy approval.[258]

7.8 Protections Against Expropriation or Nationalisation

[241] In practice, there have been very few issues of expropriation or nationalisation in Vietnam. The political regime is stable and relatively cohesive. Foreign investment is welcomed and indeed viewed as necessary, as exports from foreign-invested companies are one of the key drivers of the economy:

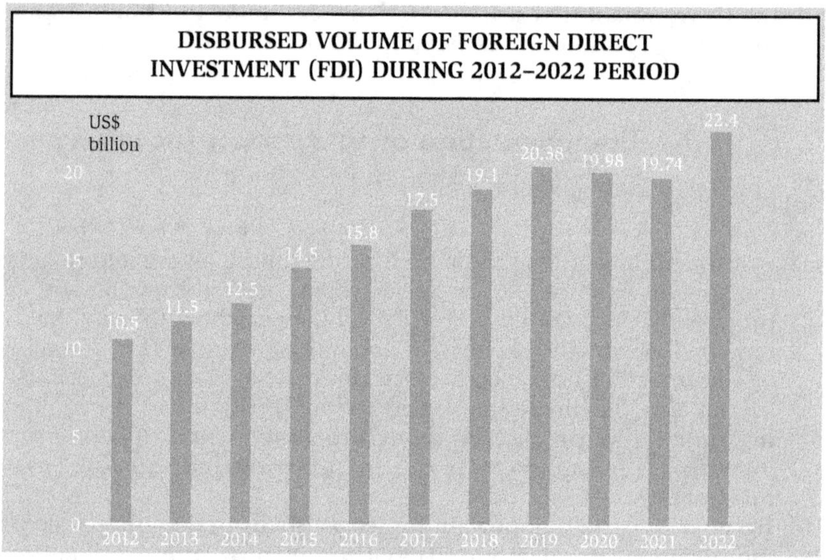

Source: website of the Vietnam Ministry of Finance.

[242] The prospects remain good, as labour costs are comparatively low, the operating environment is improving, and some important trade agreements, such as the EUVFTA and the CPTPP, have gone into effect. Any State-driven event that could be viewed as expropriation or nationalisation might upset this success and hence is viewed as unlikely to occur.[259]

---

[258] A guarantee could perhaps still be issued based on the Prime Minister's implied powers under the 2015 Law on Organisation of the Government, but this is not something in respect of which there is any formal legal position.

[259] A parallel risk – riots of a political nature – took place for the first time in mid-2014 in response to China moving an oil rig into Vietnamese waters. The effect on Chinese, Taiwanese and Singaporean

[243] In the unlikely event that there is an event that could be viewed as expropriation or nationalisation, foreign investors have some protection. The Investment Law provides that:[260]

(1) Lawful assets of investors shall not be nationalised or confiscated through administrative measures.
(2) Where the State acquires compulsorily or requisitions an asset of an investor for the reason of national defence and security, in the national interest, in emergency circumstances or for prevention of or fighting a natural calamity, such investor shall be compensated or paid in accordance with the law on compulsory acquisition and requisition of assets and other relevant laws.

7.9 Protections Against Change in Law

[244] A more difficult issue in practice for some foreign investors has been an ever-changing legal landscape, most often manifesting itself in changing tax law interpretations. This has occasionally had far-reaching consequences for investments, notably in the mining sector, which has faced new taxes that seriously affect business.

[245] Article 13 of the Investment Law and its implementing regulations provide an express guarantee to investors that:

(1) Where a new legal instrument that is promulgated provides greater investment incentives than those which the investor currently is enjoying, the investor is entitled to enjoy the investment incentives in accordance with the new legal instrument for the remaining duration in which the project is entitled to incentives.
(2) Where a new legal instrument that is promulgated provides lower investment incentives than those which the investor has previously enjoyed, the investor shall continue to be entitled to the investment incentives in accordance with the previous regulations for the remaining duration in which the project is entitled to incentives.

[246] To claim incentives under Article 13.2, an investor must demonstrate that the incentives are identified in the investment registration certificate or the investment approval.[261] Accordingly, to the extent that the incentives are important to the business and affect the decision of the buyer to invest in the target company, the target company should obtain the investment registration certificate to record the

investors was dramatic, but the Government took immediate steps to stop the rioting and to compensate the investors, and thereby restored confidence promptly. In doing so, it demonstrated the importance that foreign investment has for the economy.

[260] Article 10 of the Investment Law.

[261] Article 4.2 of Decree 31.

relevant investment incentives, even if the target is not strictly required to obtain an investment registration certificate.[262]

[247] Pursuant to Article 13.3 of the Investment Law, the investors are not entitled to the more favourable prior investment incentives if the change in the law is for reasons of national defence and security, social order and safety, social morals, the health of the community or environmental protection. In such cases, the investor can try to obtain one or more of the following:

(a) The right to deduct actual loss and damage suffered by the investor from taxable income.
(b) A change to the operational objectives of the investment project.
(c) Support to remedy loss and damage.

[248] Pursuant to Article 13.4, the above measures only become effective if the investor so requests in writing within three years after the change in law occurs.

[249] Article 13 provides a list of potential remedies without articulating a principle or providing any basis or criteria for determining which remedy should be applied in a particular case. However, Article 13 does not provide a defined basis or criteria for determining the amount of compensation or the deduction amount if such compensation or deduction were selected as the applicable remedy. Thus, if an investor decided to move forward on the basis of an Article 13 claim, it would be vulnerable to the Government making an administrative decision to 'award' the investor with relief under Article 13 with nominal compensation or an otherwise inadequate entitlement.

[250] In practice, claims under Article 13 have been rare. Where a situation has been sufficiently clear to support such a claim, the investor has usually been able to negotiate a resolution without taking the matter to formal dispute resolution.

8 FINANCING

8.1 Acquisition Financing

[251] While many target companies are leveraged, foreign buyers have usually not tapped the domestic lending market for financing. This is not likely to change swiftly for various reasons:

(a) under a new circular that comes into effect from 1 September 2023, Vietnamese banks and foreign bank branches operating in Vietnam will not be permitted to extend loans (whether short-term or long-term loans) to customers for the purpose of purchasing shares in unlisted JSCs or a capital

[262] Article 37.2 and 37.3 of the Investment Law.

contribution in LLCs.[263] To boost the real estate market, on 23 August 2023, the SBV issued another circular to postpone the application of the restriction;[264]

(b) although the restriction in subparagraph (a) does not apply to loans for purchasing listed shares or shares registered for trading on the UPCom, there are also limitations on banks in this context, including:[265]
   (i) the term of the loan must not be more than one year;
   (ii) the non-performing loan ratio of the lending bank must be lower than 3%;
   (iii) the loan cannot be secured by the shares financed by the loan; and
   (iv) the total outstanding loans to buy shares must not be higher than 5% of the charter capital of the bank.

(c) short-term acquisition financing to buy listed shares or shares registered for trading on the UPCom is complicated by the fact that the borrower may need to draw down and transfer the funds to the securities broker before the acquisition is concluded, which banks find troublesome.

[252] In light of the above, it is sometimes more practical for foreign buyers to obtain foreign loans to finance an acquisition.

8.2 Foreign Loans: Conditions and Registration

[253] Except in limited circumstances, foreign loans must be in foreign currency.[266] The borrower that generates revenues in VND will therefore take a foreign exchange risk.

[254] Short-term foreign loans are not required to be registered with the SBV, but short-term loans must not be used for long-term capital requirements.[267]

[255] Other foreign loans which must be registered with the SBV include:

(a) mid and long-term foreign loans;[268]
(b) short-term loans which have been extended such that the total term is more than one year; and

[263] Article 8.8 and 8.9 of Circular No. 39/2016/TT-NHNN on lending activities of credit institutions and branch of foreign banks to customers, as amended by Circular No. 06/2023/TT-NHNN of the SBV dated 28 Jun. 2023, effective from 1 Sep. 2023.

[264] Circular No. 10/2023/TT-NHNN of the SBV dated 23 Aug. 2023, effective from 01 Sep. 2023.

[265] Article 12 of Circular 22/2019/TT-NHNN of the SBV dated 15 Nov. 2019 (as amended on 1 Oct. 2020 and 31 Dec. 2022) on prudential ratios applicable to banks and foreign bank branches.

[266] Article 7 of Circular 12/2014/TT-NHNN of the SBV dated 31 Mar. 2014 (as amended on 15 Aug. 2017) providing requirements of foreign loans of enterprises which are not guaranteed by the Government (***Circular 12/2014***). From 15 Aug. 2023, Circular 12/2014 will be replaced by Circular 08/2023/TT-NHNN of the SBV dated 30 Jun. 2023 (***Circular 08***). Article 10.2 of Circular 08 is more relaxed and allows the parties to denominate the repayment obligations in VND.

[267] Article 11.1(a) of Circular 12/2014. Article 17.1(a) of Circular 08 only permits a Vietnamese company to borrow short-term loans to (i) repay other offshore loans or (ii) repay short-term debts.

[268] Short-term loans are those with a term of 1 year or less.

(c) short-term loans which have not been extended but which have not been fully paid within 30 days from the first anniversary of the first disbursement.[269]

[256] A failure to register the loan agreement, or any changes to it, with the SBV could preclude the borrower from obtaining foreign exchange to repay the loan and/or remit the money offshore for such repayment.

8.3 Foreign Loans: Tax and Transfer Pricing

[257] Foreign contractor taxes are levied on foreign organisations which have no permanent presence in Vietnam but which conduct business in Vietnam or have income arising in Vietnam.[270] The result is that payment of interest to foreign lenders is subject to a withholding tax of 5%, except if there is double tax avoidance treaty protection.[271]

[258] Vietnam is becoming increasingly focused on transfer pricing issues, so unrealistic interest rates paid to shareholders or other related parties could be penalised. This can occur through direct investigation and formal penalties, difficulties with obtaining licences and approvals, and damage to reputation through media campaigns against foreign companies suspected of not paying enough tax.

8.4 Foreign Loans: Offshore Bank Accounts

[259] Local companies can open offshore bank accounts provided that they obtain a licence from the SBV to do so.[272] Permission is usually only granted to companies that (i) have an overseas branch or representative office; or (ii) need to open offshore bank accounts to receive foreign loans or implement undertakings and contracts with foreign parties.

---

[269] Article 11 of Circular 12/2022/TT-NHNN of the SBV dated 30 Sep. 2022 providing guidelines on foreign exchange management with respect to borrowing and repayment of foreign loans by enterprises.

[270] Circular 103/2014/TT-BTC of the MOF dated 6 Aug. 2014 guiding the performance of tax obligations applicable to foreign organisations and individuals doing business or earning income in Vietnam (***Circular 103***).

[271] Article 13.2(a) of Circular 103. France is one of the few countries with a tax treaty that may provide some protection in some circumstances.

[272] Article 12.1 of Decree 70/2014/ND-CP of the Government dated 17 Jul. 2014 providing details of implementation of a number of articles of the Foreign Exchange Ordinance and Ordinance amending and supplementing the Foreign Exchange Ordinance (***Foreign Exchange Ordinance***); Circular 20/2015/TT-NHNN of the SBV dated 28 Oct. 2015 on opening and using overseas bank accounts of institutional residents.

8.5 Debt Limitations

[260] Debt of foreign-owned companies can be limited by the fact that such companies cannot borrow mid-term and long-term loans to implement an investment project in an amount greater than the difference between the investment capital and the charter capital set out in its investment registration certificate for that investment project.[273]

8.6 Security Interests

(a) Security Interests: General

[261] The financing of projects in Vietnam is complicated by a security interest regime which, though much improved, is largely untested in terms of enforcement.

[262] Although a lender can take security over shares, bank accounts, land and buildings, movables and receivables in the form of a mortgage or a pledge, the range of security interests available under Vietnamese law is limited in comparison with other jurisdictions. Some forms of security available in other jurisdictions, such as collateral assignments, charges, trusts and liens, are not recognised under Vietnamese law.

[263] The Civil Code of Vietnam permits various forms of security interests for business obligations, namely mortgages, pledges, guarantees, performance bonds, security deposits, escrow accounts, title retention and possessory liens.[274] Under the Civil Code:

(i) a pledge is an arrangement pursuant to which the pledgor hands over the possession of an asset to the pledgee as security for the performance of an obligation;[275]
(ii) a mortgage is an arrangement pursuant to which the mortgagor uses its assets without handing over the possession of such assets as security for the performance of an obligation;[276] and
(iii) a guarantee is an arrangement pursuant to which the guarantor undertakes to the beneficiary to perform an obligation on behalf of an obligor if the obligation falls due and the obligor fails to perform, or improperly performs, the obligation.[277]

[264] The definitions of a mortgage and a pledge under the Civil Code give rise to some confusion in relation to whether a mortgage or a pledge is appropriate for

[273] Article 11.2(b) of Circular 12/2014. Similar provision is provided under Art. 18.1 of Circular 08.
[274] Article 292 of the Civil Code.
[275] Article 309 of the Civil Code.
[276] Article 317 of the Civil Code.
[277] Article 335 of the Civil Code.

certain forms of property, including intangible property such as accounts receivable, deposit accounts and intellectual property rights, because these properties cannot be physically handed over or retained.

[265] Article 33 of Decree 21[278] suggests that a security interest over the right to claim a debt (which may include accounts receivable) should be created through a mortgage. However, the right to claim a debt is but one example of an intangible that cannot be physically handed over to another party.

[266] Because the Civil Code governs transactions entered into by both foreigners (e.g., foreign lenders) and Vietnamese companies, the Civil Code is seen as conferring the right on foreign lenders to take mortgages, pledges and guarantees. Foreign investors are specifically entitled to mortgage their shares in local companies to secure their obligations.

(b) Security Interests: Mortgages of Assets

[267] Under the Civil Code, a mortgage may be granted over both movable and immovable assets. In general, companies cannot grant mortgages of land use rights and the property attached to the land to foreigners.[279] Please refer to section 8.6(f) 'Security Interests: Land use Rights and Assets Attached to Land'. Apart from that, the right of foreign lenders to take security over Vietnamese assets is generally unrestricted.[280]

(c) Security Interests: Mortgages of Equity Interests

[268] As assignments by way of security are not recognised under Vietnamese law, a security interest over an investor's equity in a company takes the form of a mortgage or pledge. The enforcement of a transfer of an equity interest in a non-public Vietnamese company may require an acquisition approval, an amended enterprise registration certificate and/or an investment registration certificate reflecting the completion of the transfer by the licensing authority. In some large transactions, lenders have required not only that the security interest itself be approved by a governmental authority but also that their right to transfer an equity interest on enforcement be pre-approved by the licensing authorities. In practice, the licensing authorities are not generally prepared to give such pre-approval.

(d) Security Interests: Guarantees

[269] Vietnamese law treats a guarantee as a type of security, but a guarantee does not grant the secured party automatic recourse to specific property of the

[278] Decree No. 21/2021/ND-CP of the Government dated 19 Mar. 2021 on security transactions (***Decree 21***).

[279] Article 183 of the Land Law.

[280] Article 105 of the Civil Code states that '*property comprises tangible things, money or valuable papers and property rights*'. Of course, if a particular asset, such as listed shares or shares in some regulated companies, is not permitted to be owned by a foreigner, then upon enforcement, the foreign lender will have to transfer possession of such collateral to a person entitled to own it rather than to take possession of the collateral itself.

guarantor.[281] Specific property of the guarantor would only be used as collateral if the guarantor provides a pledge or mortgage.

(e) Security Interests: Third-party security

[270] Vietnamese law seems to recognise the concept of third-party security. Articles 3.1 and 3.3 of Decree 21 make a distinction between a 'securing party' and an 'obligor' that owes the obligation. These two persons are not necessarily the same.' Article 4.3 of Decree 21 goes on to provide that '*the owner of the assets and the secured party must apply the regulations on pledge and mortgage of assets if they agree to use assets as security for performance of the obligation of another person.*' These provisions suggest that the owner may grant security over its assets to secure the obligations of a third-party obligor.

[271] However, several courts and judges in Vietnam in practice have taken the view that a mortgage over assets by a third party as security for the obligations of others is invalid and unenforceable. In light of this, the security granted by the third party could be structured as a limited non-recourse guarantee which is secured by a pledge or mortgage over the assets of a third party. This structure is supported by Article 43 of Decree 21, which provides that 'the parties to a guarantee may agree on the establishment of a security transaction to secure the performance of a guaranteed obligation, and on the obligation the principal owes to the guarantor in accordance with laws'.

[272] The limited guarantee structure however gives rise to another issue if the obligor is an offshore company. Currently, a Vietnamese resident cannot provide a guarantee for the obligations of a non-resident unless the Prime Minister's approval is obtained.[282] The Prime Minister does not give such approval lightly, and we are only aware of such approval having been issued to SOEs conducting overseas investments.

[273] Foreign creditors will also face the risk that foreign exchange regulations do not provide a basis for a Vietnamese resident to pay foreign creditors under the third-party security arrangement.

(f) Security Interests: Land Use Rights and Assets Attached to Land

[274] Companies are permitted to:

(i) grant mortgages over land use rights and assets attached to land to credit institutions operating in Vietnam if (A) they have been allocated the land and have paid the land use fee, or (B) they have leased the land and have paid the land rent for the entire lease term;[283] and

[281] Article 43.1 of Decree 21 provides that '*the parties to a guarantee may agree on establishment of a security transaction to secure the performance of a guaranteed obligation.*'

[282] Article 17.3 of the Foreign Exchange Ordinance.

[283] Article 183.3 of the Land Law

(ii) grant mortgages over assets attached to land (not land use rights) to credit institutions operating in Vietnam if they have leased the land and pay annual land rent as it comes due.[284]

[275] Foreign lenders cannot take a mortgage of land use rights[285] or assets attached to land.[286] Although it is debatable, this may extend to branches of foreign banks operating in Vietnam.[287]

(g) Security Interests: Security Over Future Assets

[276] Security can be granted over 'future assets'.[288] 'Future assets' include: (i) assets that are not yet created; and (ii) assets already formed whose ownership must be registered but which can only be registered after entering into the security transaction.[289]

(h) Security Interests: Registration of Security Interests

[277] Certain security interests must be registered in order to be effective, including:

(i) mortgages must be registered with the land registration office if they involve (A) land use rights, (B) houses and assets attached to land which have been recorded in the ownership certificate, and (C) housing or construction projects, agricultural or forest projects, and other projects using land allocated by the State or leased from the State with pre-payment for the entire lease term;[290] and

(ii) pledges and mortgages of aircraft,[291] which must be registered with the Civil Aviation Administration of Vietnam.[292]

[278] It is not completely clear if mortgages of sea-going ships must be registered in order to be effective. Unlike its predecessor,[293] Decree 99 does not specifically require a mortgage over sea-going vessels to be registered, nor does the Maritime Law.[294] However, it would be prudent for a creditor to require the obligor to register the mortgage over the sea-going vessel to create priority over the asset.

---

284 Article 183.2 of the Land Law.

285 Article 183 of the Land Law.

286 There are no clear statements in Vietnamese law as to whether immovable assets on land may be mortgaged separately from a mortgage over the relevant land use rights. Nevertheless, the provisions of the Land Law would prevent a foreign lender from taking a mortgage over the assets attached to the land.

287 Under the 1997 Law on Credit Institutions, land and assets attached to land could be mortgaged in favour of credit institutions operating in Vietnam. However, the 2010 Law on Credit Institutions draws a distinction between credit institutions and foreign bank branches, thus calling into question the ability of a foreign bank branch to take a mortgage over land.

288 Articles 8 and 24 of Decree 21.

289 Article 108.2 of the Civil Code.

290 Article 25.1 of Decree 99/2022/ND-CP of the Government dated 30 Nov. 2021 on registration of secured transaction (***Decree 99***).

291 Article 29.1 through Art. 28.1(c) of the Law on Aviation.

292 Article 38 of Decree 99.

293 Article 4.1(d) of Decree 102/2017/ND-CP of the Government dated 1 Sep. 2017 on registration of secured transactions.

294 Article 37 of Law on Maritime of the National Assembly dated 25 Nov. 2015.

Mortgages over sea-going vessels are registered with the provincial maritime bureau or seaport authority under the Vietnam National Maritime Bureau.[295]

[279] Although not compulsory, certain other security interests can be registered at the request of the parties, including:

(i) mortgages of (A) houses or other assets attached to land formed in the future and (B) assets attached to land that are not subject to ownership registration requirements and are not recorded in the ownership certificate, which can be registered with the land department;[296]
(ii) (A) mortgages of movable assets, (B) retention of title to movable assets, (C) pledges, performance bonds, security deposits or escrow accounts over or by movable assets, (D) security interests in securities unregistered with the VSD or (E) security interests in temporary assets attached to land, which can be registered with the National Authority for Registration of Secured Transactions;[297]
(iii) security over shares that have been registered with the VSD can be registered with the VSD.[298]

[280] Cautious lenders require borrowers to register all registrable security interests because if any subsequent security interest is registered first, it will have priority over registrable security interests which have not been registered or which are registered later.[299]

(i) Security Interests: Foreclosure

[281] The parties to security documents can agree on the enforcement methods, including by way of:[300]

(i) public auction;
(ii) private sale (including the right to sell to itself);
(iii) in respect of security over accounts, withdrawal of amounts standing to the credit of the accounts;
(iv) receipt of direct payments from third parties; or
(v) taking possession and becoming the owner of the security assets in substitution for the performance of the mortgagor's or the borrower's obligations.

[282] If there is no agreement on enforcement methods, then the secured assets have to be sold by way of public auction.[301] It is therefore important to specify the enforcement methods in the security agreement.

---

[295] Article 41 of Decree 99.
[296] Article 25.2 of Decree 99.
[297] Article 44.1 of Decree 99.
[298] Chapter V of Decree 155.
[299] Article 308 through Art. 297 of the Civil Code.
[300] Article 303.1 of the Civil Code.
[301] Article 303.2 of the Civil Code. Article 52.2 of Decree 21 provides that if the parties agree that enforcement can be via auction, they can agree on the procedures for such auction. If they do not have an agreement on the subject, the auction process would follow the general auction laws. If there is no agreement on enforcement methods, and if the secured assets are listed securities, or other

[283] Upon the occurrence of an event of default, a lender would be entitled to foreclose by taking physical possession of the secured assets without the need for judicial proceedings or the permission of a court or other official body. If the party holding the secured property failed to deliver the secured property to the lender, the lender could theoretically seize the security property, or it could request a court to resolve the matter.[302]

[284] In practice, a lender may need a court judgment. However, the courts of Vietnam can be unpredictable and unsatisfactory. And even if a lender obtained a favourable judgment from a court, the enforceability of such judgment in practice would be uncertain.

9 PAYMENT, FOREIGN EXCHANGE AND REMITTANCE

9.1 General

[285] The foreign exchange regulations distinguish between enterprises with foreign direct investment capital (***FDI enterprises***) and others (***non-FDI enterprises***).

[286] Under the foreign exchange regulations, an FDI enterprise is, in broad terms:[303]

(a) a non-public enterprise established by foreign investors which have had to obtain an investment registration certificate; or
(b) a non-public enterprise more than 51% owned by foreign investors; or
(c) a non-public project company established by foreign investors to implement public-private projects (PPP).

9.2 Accounts and Payment for Acquisitions of Shares in an FDI Enterprise

[287] FDI enterprises have to open a direct investment capital account (***DICA***) in foreign currency (and may open one in Vietnamese Dong as well). This account is used for the receipt of capital contributions as well as the repatriation of direct investment capital, profit and other legal revenues overseas.[304]

[288] The purchase price for acquisitions of shares or equity interests in FDI enterprises:[305]

movable assets whose price can be determined by reference to a market, such assets would be sold on the stock exchange or other relevant exchange (Art. 52.3 of Decree 21).

302 Article 52.5 and 52.6 of Decree 21.

303 Article 3.2 of Circular 06/2019/TT-NHNN of the SBV dated 26 Jun. 2019 providing guidance on foreign exchange control with respect to foreign direct investment activities (***Circular 06***).

304 Articles 5.2 and 6.2 of Circular 06.

305 Article 10 of Circular 06.

(a) must be made (in Vietnamese Dong) through the DICA if either the buyer or the seller is a resident and the other is a non-resident;
(b) does not have to be made through the DICA if both the buyer and the seller are non-residents. In this case, payment for the purchase of shares may be made in foreign currency. It is widely understood that payment, in this case, can either be made (x) through a foreign currency account opened in Vietnam or (y) offshore.

[289] Payments for many acquisitions of shares or equity interests in FDI enterprises in the latter case have been made offshore. However, a few vigilant foreign buyers chose to make payments through a foreign currency account opened in Vietnam at a licensed bank. This is because it is easier for the buyers to procure evidence to show to Vietnamese authorities (e.g., tax authorities or the DPI) that they have legitimately invested in Vietnam (bank statements evidencing the payment issued by a Vietnamese bank are apparently easier to procure and more convincing to authorities than those issued by a foreign bank).

9.3 Accounts and Payment for Acquisitions of Shares in Non-FDI Enterprises

[290] All investments in non-FDI enterprises by non-resident foreign investors must be conducted in Vietnamese Dong via one (and only one) indirect investment capital account (***IICA***) held by the investor at an authorised bank.[306]

[291] Foreign investors are prohibited from transferring amounts in their IICAs into term deposits or savings deposits. If an investor wishes to remit capital or profit, it is entitled to use the Vietnamese Dong in its IICA to purchase foreign currency from a bank.

[292] Payment for the purchase of shares in non-FDI enterprises must be made in Vietnamese Dong.[307]

9.4 Remitting Foreign Currency: Investing in FDI Enterprises

[293] FDI enterprises are entitled to transfer profit and other legitimate income abroad through the DICA.[308] There is no guarantee that there is foreign currency available for such conversion in the banking system.

---

[306] Circular 05/2014/TT-NHNN of the SBV dated 12 Mar. 2014 on opening and using indirect investment capital accounts for indirect investment activities in Vietnam (***Circular 05***).
[307] Article 4.1 of Circular 05.
[308] Article 11 of the Foreign Exchange Ordinance; Arts 5.2 and 6.2 of Circular 06.

[294] FDI enterprises can remit their profits abroad on an annual basis or upon termination of their investment in Vietnam, not on a quarterly or half-yearly basis as previously permitted.[309]

[295] The purchase of foreign currency and its remittance offshore, including the remittance of money in the DICA after a sale of an investor's interests in an FDI enterprise, is governed by foreign exchange control regulations. The foreign investor will have to submit certain documents to the bank in order to be able to effect the transfer of funds, including certification of fulfilment of tax obligations.

9.5 Remitting Foreign Currency: Investing in Non-FDI Enterprises

[296] Foreign investors that have made investments in non-FDI enterprises in Vietnam are entitled to use Vietnamese Dong in their IICA to buy foreign currency and transfer such amounts abroad.[310] There is no guarantee in the law that there will be foreign currency available in the banking system. In practice, banks have occasionally in the past been reluctant to sell US Dollars to foreign investors for remittance offshore. Any delay could result in devaluation in the earnings or sales proceeds of foreign investors in foreign exchange terms. However, this has been extremely rare in practice.

10 COMPANY LAW AND SECURITIES LAW ISSUES

10.1 Shareholder Approvals

[297] Shareholder approvals for the purchase of secondary shares in a JSC would be needed in certain situations:

(a) if an outside buyer purchases secondary shares from a founding shareholder of the target company within three years after the establishment of the target company, the general meeting of shareholders will have to approve the sale of the shares to the buyer;[311]
(b) to avoid a mandatory PTO; and
(c) the charter of a company includes the requirement for shareholder approval. This is rare in practice, especially for public companies.

---

309 Circular 186/2010/TT-BTC of the MOF dated 18 Nov. 2010 providing guidelines for transfer abroad of profits of foreign organisation and individuals from direct investment in Vietnam in accordance with the investment law (***Circular 186***).

310 Article 12 of the Foreign Exchange Ordinance. Article 7.2 of Circular 05.

311 During the three-year period after the issuance of a enterprise registration certificate, ordinary shares of a founding shareholder can only be transferred to other founding shareholders. Any sale of such shares to outside investors must be approved at the general meeting of shareholders. Article 120.3 of the Enterprise Law.

10.2 Regulatory Approvals

[298]

(a) A foreign investor must obtain acquisition approval from the DPI in order to:[312]
  (i) invest in a non-public company that is engaged in, or authorised to engage in, a business where a 'market access condition' is applicable to foreign investors;
  (ii) acquire an interest in a non-public company that takes foreign ownership of more than 50% of the charter capital; or
  (iii) acquire an interest in a non-public company having land in certain border, coastal or national defence and security locations.
(b) Before an acquisition approval would be granted to a foreign purchaser', a pre-approval (or established policy) from the ministry responsible for such line of business would be required.[313]
(c) If a foreign investor acquires an interest in a foreign-invested company, an amendment to the investment registration certificate would also be required.[314]
(d) Changes in the ownership interest in a Vietnamese company require various notifications and registrations.[315]
(e) The acquisition of shares in a public company may be subject to certain approvals or require notifications and registrations.[316]

10.3 Governance Issues

(a) Governance

[299] It is not uncommon to encounter issues related to corporate governance deficiencies, problematic corporate structures and opaque ownership structures. Popular problems relate to:

(i) Nominee ownership structures – It is not unusual for shares to be owned by nominees, such that control is in effect exercised by persons who are not apparent on the title.[317]
(ii) Accounting irregularities – Certain Vietnamese companies may keep two (or more) sets of accounts, which could have tax and other consequences.

---

312 *See* section 'Regulatory framework'.

313 *See* discussion in section 'Government and Political System' for more details.

314 *See* para. (d) of section of 'Regulatory framework'.

315 *See* section 'Compliance and reporting requirements'.

316 *See* section 'Public Company Acquisitions'.

317 Under the current Investment Law, there are even greater risks in nominee arrangements. *See* section 'Acquisitions of Interests Through Nominees'.

(iii) Conflicts – there is often no clear distinction between personal interest and corporate interest from the founders' perspective. It is not uncommon for Vietnamese companies to have no internal control system to screen for and prevent conflicts of interest. After closing, it is often necessary to implement a system of effective internal controls to detect and prevent conflicts of interest, though this may be met with resistance. If possible, agreement on internal control implementation should be included in the transaction documents. Like other improvements to corporate governance, if presented in the right way, as value creation, this otherwise contentious area can play to the strengths of potential acquirers.

[300] Because the success of many acquisitions will depend on changes and other improvements to corporate governance and/or management, to increase the chances of a successful deal, it is important to understand the target company's culture and the personalities of the management team and use this understanding.

[301] Two-way education and due diligence between the buyer and seller about the culture of the respective organisations may be useful in raising awareness of potential cultural differences and may allow the parties to think proactively about ways to deal with such difficulties. To the extent that a change or improvement is needed, such change should be clearly communicated to the investee company's management. If possible, the management should be incentivised to achieve the change and improvement.

(b) Loyalty

[302] The Enterprise Law requires directors and managers[318] to be loyal to the interests of the company and its shareholders. They must not use information (including information about a proposed acquisition) or business opportunities of the company, or abuse their position in the company, for their own purposes or for the benefit of any other party.[319]

(c) Inside Information

[303] Directors are deemed to have access to the inside information[320] of a public company. They must not use it to buy or sell securities for themselves or others, and must not disclose or supply inside information to others or advise others to buy or sell securities based on the inside information.[321] The effectiveness of these strictures in practice has sometimes been questioned.

[318] These include members of the members' council, the president or chairman of an LLC, the members of the board of a JSC, the general director, the inspector, and other managerial positions as set out in a company's charter.

[319] Articles 13.1(b), 71.1(b), 83.3, 97.3, 107.3, 165.1(c) and 173.3 of the Enterprise Law.

[320] Inside information is defined as undisclosed information relating to a public company which once disclosed may have a great impact on the price of the securities of such public company. There is no further light on what this means. In practice, this is not an area that seems to have been at the forefront of the regulators' agenda.

[321] Article 12.2 of the Securities Law. *See* discussion in section 'Governing Law'.

(d) Tender Offers

[304] Directors have various obligations in the context of a tender offer.[322] For example, if a public company receives a tender offer, it must publish the relevant information within three days from the date of such receipt.[323] Within ten days from the date of receipt, the board of the target public company must send information on the tender offer (together with opinions of the target public company) to the SSC and shareholders of such company.[324]

10.4 Form of Consideration

[305] Contributions in kind in return for the initial issuance of shares are allowed under the Enterprise Law. Assets that are contributed in kind at the time of establishment have to be valued by the founding shareholders or by a professional valuation agency.[325] If approval is granted by the founding shareholders, it must be unanimous. In the latter case, the value of the capital contribution must be approved by more than 50% of the founding shareholders. If the value of a contributed asset is overestimated, all founding shareholders would be jointly liable for the debts and other liabilities of the company to the extent of the excess over the actual value.[326]

[306] Assets used for the contribution of capital after the initial establishment of a company may be valued: (i) by agreement between the company and the contributing shareholder; or (ii) by a professional valuation service (the valuation of the valuation company is subject to approval by the company and the contributing shareholder). If the value of the contributed asset is overestimated, the contributing shareholder and the board of the company would be jointly liable for any loss and damage caused.[327]

[307] There are no restrictions on the subsequent disposal of shares purchased by a contribution in kind.

[308] Public companies can issue shares in return for the receipt of other shares.[328] There have been some domestic share-for-share deals, including:

(i) the issuance of shares by FPT for swapping shares in its subsidiary companies in 2011;
(ii) the issuance of shares by Kinh Do Company in order to purchase shares of Vinabico in June 2013;

[322] *See* section 'Public Company Acquisitions' for more detail.
[323] Article 86.2 of Decree 155.
[324] Article 87.1 of Decree 155.
[325] Article 36.2 of the Enterprise Law.
[326] *Ibid.*
[327] Article 36.3 of the Enterprise Law.
[328] Article 49 of Decree 155.

(iii) share swap in relation to the merger of Mekong Housing Bank (***MHB***) into Bank for Investment and Development of Vietnam (***BIDV***) in May 2015; and
(iv) the merger of VinCommerce into Masan Consumer Holding in 2019.

[309] Most of these deals have involved listed shares whose market value could be relatively easily determined.

[310] However, it is much more difficult to undertake a share swap in respect of shares of non-public companies, especially in case of cross-border transactions.[329] In practice, the overwhelming majority of acquisitions are for cash. Where, as is often the case, the complexities or uncertainties of share-for-share deals are too great, parties have achieved similar results through cash round-trips or netting arrangements.

10.5 Financial Assistance

[311] A public company must not extend loans or issue guarantees to or for the benefit of shareholders and related persons, except for limited circumstances.[330] Apart from this, Vietnamese law generally does not prohibit a grant of security by a company in a target group to secure a loan to another company in Vietnam.

10.6 Purchase of Own Shares

[312] A company may be able to redeem its ordinary shares, but the situations are limited primarily to (i) a demand of a shareholder (if such shareholder has voted against a decision of a shareholders' meeting on the reorganisation of the company or change of rights and obligations of the shareholders), or (ii) a decision of such company on a pro-rata redemption (but in this case, the maximum redemption is 30% of the total outstanding ordinary shares of such company).[331] A company may only pay shareholders for redeemed shares if after such payment the company is still able to pay off all its debts and liabilities.[332] If payment for redeemed shares results in a decrease in the total book value of the company's assets by more than 10%, the company must notify all of its creditors within fifteen days after the date of such payment.[333]

[329] To pave the way for future fund raising or IPO, there is a recent trend that companies in Vietnam are reorganised such that there is a new parent company of the group in another jurisdiction (e.g., Singapore) and the shareholders of the Vietnamese companies become shareholders of the new parent company.

[330] Article 293 of Decree 155.

[331] Articles 132 and 133 of the Enterprise Law.

[332] Article 134.1 of the Enterprise Law.

[333] Article 134.4 of the Enterprise Law.

[313] The redemption of preference shares can be easier. For example, redeemable preference shares can be redeemed according to their terms.[334] A company may redeem up to 100% of dividend preference shares at a redemption price agreed between the parties.[335] A public company is subject to various requirements and restrictions when redeeming its shares, including:

(a) the General Meeting of Shareholders of the public company must approve the reduction of charter capital and the share redemption plan, which specifies the number, the timeline and the principles to be used to determine the purchase price;[336]
(b) the funds used for share redemptions must be capital surplus, investment development funds, undistributed profit after taxes, or other equity funds for capital increases;
(c) a securities company must be appointed to conduct a share redemption, except when the redemption is by a securities company that is a member of the Stock Exchange of Vietnam;[337]
(d) it must satisfy the relevant conditions if it has conditional business lines;[338]
(e) a public company can redeem its shares without complying with the foregoing conditions if:[339]
    (i) the redemption is required by the shareholders in accordance with the Enterprise Law;
    (ii) the redemption is of shares of employees issued in accordance with an employee stock option plan;
    (iii) the redemption is meant to fix a transaction error or is an odd lot buyback.
(f) a public company must not redeem shares in the following cases:[340]
    (i) it has overdue debts according to the latest audited financial statements;
    (ii) it is in the course of issuing more shares;
    (iii) its shares are subject to a PTO; or
    (iv) it has redeemed shares or issued new shares in the previous six months.

[314] Under the new Securities Law, public companies can no longer keep treasury shares. Shares that have been redeemed will have to be cancelled, and charter capital will be reduced accordingly.[341] Shares that had been redeemed before 1 January 2021 can be kept in treasury for distribution as bonus shares.[342]

---

[334] Article 118.1 of the Enterprise Law.
[335] Article 133 of the Enterprise Law.
[336] Article 36.1(a) of the Securities Law.
[337] Article 36.1(c) of the Securities Law.
[338] Article 36.1(d) of the Securities Law.
[339] Article 36.2 of the Securities Law.
[340] Article 36.3 of the Securities Law.
[341] Article 36.5 of the Securities Law.
[342] Article 310.4 of Decree 155.

10.7 Preference Shares

[315] The Enterprise Law contemplates four types of preference shares:[343]

(i) dividend preference shares (non-voting);
(ii) voting preference shares;
(iii) redeemable preference shares (non-voting); and
(iv) other preference shares as stipulated in a company's charter and the securities laws.

[316] Preference shares can be converted into ordinary shares pursuant to a shareholders' resolution. Ordinary shares may not be converted into preference shares.

[317] There is almost no law relating to preference shares in Vietnam, there are limited preference share precedents, and there has been no practice relating to the enforcement in court of preference share rights by foreign shareholders.

[318] As a result of the lack of a law on preference shares, there are no answers to numerous questions about how they would work, and the licensing authorities (i.e., the local DPIs) are currently very rigid when registering changes in the charter capital of a company resulting from the redemption of preference shares. That has not deterred more and more companies from using such shares.

(a) Dividend Preferences

[319] At law, dividend preference shares are entitled either to dividends at a rate higher than those paid on ordinary shares or to an annual fixed-rate dividend. The fixed dividend is paid irrespective of the performance of the company. The law states that dividends on preference shares can be paid in accordance with the conditions applicable to them.[344] This implies that payment can be made not just out of profit (as is the case for ordinary shares) but also out of cash flow, capital or any combination thereof.

[320] Sometimes, an investor's dividend preference is not absolutely fixed at an annual Vietnamese Dong amount, as adjustments may occur, including in respect of the exchange rate. But if the amount of the dividend is calculated on an annual basis and is fixed by the terms of the preference share rights in the charter, it can be argued that this should be deemed to be a fixed rate dividend that is acceptable at law.

(b) Liquidation Preference

[321] Vietnamese law does not preclude the issuance of liquidation preference shares. Nor does it specifically contemplate them. Any issuance of liquidation preference shares by a company would be based on a company's power to issue preference shares in the fourth category mentioned above (i.e., other preference shares set out in its charter).[345]

---

[343] Article 114.2 of the Enterprise Law.

[344] Article 117.1 of the Enterprise Law.

[345] There is another interpretation that in order to be qualified to be preference shares in the fourth category mentioned above, those shares must be stipulated in both (i) a company's charter and (ii) the

[322] Under the Enterprise Law, ordinary shareholders have the right to receive part of the assets remaining in a bankruptcy or dissolution of a company in proportion to the capital contributed by them. It is unclear if this could be interpreted to refer to all capital rather than just the capital contributed by ordinary shareholders. If the former, then a liquidation preference is arguably illegal or at least ineffective.

(c) Hybrid Preference Shares

[323] A company may issue other preference shares as stipulated in a company's charter and the securities laws. Practitioners commonly interpret this to mean that a corporate charter may provide for any preference rights other than dividend preference shares, voting preference shares or redeemable preference shares. However, because the law does not specify whether it is permissible to have a class of preference shares that overlaps with, but is not consistent with, those classes specifically enumerated in the law (e.g., the law does not contemplate hybrid classes or state whether the 'other' class of preference shares can include elements of the specifically permitted classes), it is not clear how enforceable hybrids involving dividend preferences, voting preferences or redemption preferences would be in practice.

10.8 Shareholders' Agreements

[324] Vietnamese law does not contain any specific legal basis for a shareholders' agreement, nor does it prohibit shareholders' agreements. There are general provisions in the law that in theory cover shareholders' agreements, including the right of Vietnamese companies to act 'autonomously', recognition of the principle of freedom of contract and a general catch-all that contracts that are not forbidden by law and not contrary to 'social ethics' are generally permitted.

[325] However, the law also confers equal rights, obligations and benefits on all shareholders of the same class of shares in a Vietnamese company, which can create ambiguity around the enforceability of some parts of certain shareholders' agreements if they are not carefully drafted. Depending on the specific issues, it may be prudent to consider separate classes of shares, though this is not always possible or advisable. It may also be advisable to separate rights relating to the company (which should be covered to the extent possible in the company's charter) from rights negotiated between shareholders relating to the transfer of their shares and similar matters.

[326] Notwithstanding the above, shareholders' agreements are commonly used in the market.

securities laws. And because the securities laws do not stipulate any type of preference shares, a company cannot issue preference shares in the fourth category. This interpretation is too strict as it effectively makes the relevant provision of the Enterprise Law meaningless.

10.9 Restrictions on Transferability of Shares

[327] The Enterprise Law confers on a shareholder of a Vietnamese JSC the right to 'freely assign their shares to other shareholders and non-shareholders' (with limited exceptions). Therefore, there is a risk that provisions in a charter such as lock-ups, pre-emptive rights, rights of first refusal/offer and other transfer restrictions may not be enforced by a Vietnamese court in the event of a dispute. While this risk is much higher in the case of public companies, the risk in respect of non-public companies is limited because the law itself contemplates many such restrictions in specific contexts.

[328] As a practical matter, transfer restrictions are frequently seen in the market and market participants generally act on the assumption that transfer restrictions are enforceable.

10.10 Put and Call Agreements

[329] Put and call options have few legal underpinnings and are largely untested in Vietnam. That being said, foreign investors have employed put and call options in the market, and there have been instances where the exercise of a call option proceeded without any significant issues.

[330] As with any transfer of shares in a Vietnamese company, regulatory approvals are typically required. Therefore, the exercise of a put or call option is rarely self-executing, and even if the shares are held in escrow or are otherwise 'controlled', there will be interaction with a regulator that has broad discretion to approve or disapprove any transaction or to ask for more information and/or further documentation.

10.11 Costs and Fees

[331] For foreign buyers, the main costs (excluding professional advisory fees) arise out of the need, in most cases, to obtain approval for the acquisition from the provincial DPI and an amendment to the investment registration certificate. There are no official fees for such approvals, but the cost of preparing the documents for registration/application is often significant. The opportunity costs of the delays that are often inherent in the process can also be appreciable.

10.12 Dividends

[332] Dividends can be distributed to investors provided that the following conditions have been met:[346]

[346] Article 69 in respect of LLCs; Article 135.2 of the Enterprise Law in respect of JSCs.

(a) the company has generated a profit;
(b) the company has fulfilled its tax and other financial obligations to Vietnam;
(c) the company has set up such funds as may be required under its charter;
(d) the company has fully recouped any losses of previous financial years; and
(e) debts and other liabilities may be paid in full after the distribution.

[333] There are certain restrictions on the timing of dividend payments by a JSC. The dividends must be fully paid within six months from the end of the relevant annual general shareholders' meeting.[347] There is no restriction on the timing of payment of dividends by an LLC.

[334] A foreign investor would be permitted to transfer profits overseas in the following circumstances:

(a) an annual transfer of dividends after the end of the company's fiscal year provided that the Vietnamese company: (i) has fulfilled its financial obligations to the State; and (ii) has submitted audited financial statements and declaration of CIT for such fiscal year to the relevant tax authority;[348] and
(b) a final transfer upon the sale of its investment in Vietnam provided that the company: (i) has fulfilled its financial obligations to the State; (ii) has submitted the audited financial statement and the declaration of CIT for the latest fiscal year to the relevant tax authority; and (iii) has fulfilled all obligations under the law on tax management.[349]

[335] The amount of the annual dividend that can be transferred overseas is the amount of profit distributed to the foreign investor for the financial year based on audited financial statements and the CIT finalisation declaration of the Vietnamese company (in addition to other profit, such as profit carried forward from previous years and not previously distributed), less: (i) items which the foreign investor has used or undertaken to use to reinvest in Vietnam, and (ii) profit distributions which the foreign investor has used to pay for its needs in Vietnam.[350]

10.13 Corporate Veil

[336] Parent companies are generally only responsible for the debts and liabilities of their subsidiaries to the extent of capital that has to be contributed to such subsidiaries. However, there are exceptions in respect of an incorrect withdrawal of capital, fraud, improper related-party transactions and a failure to respect the corporate individuality of the subsidiary.

[347] Article 135.4 of the Enterprise Law.
[348] Article 4.1 of Circular 186.
[349] Article 4.2 of Circular 186.
[350] Article 3.1 of Circular 186.

10.14 Bankruptcy

[337] According to the World Bank's 2020 Ease of Doing Business Report, Vietnam ranked 122 out of 190 for resolving insolvency. The report noted that it still takes, on average, five years to conclude a bankruptcy case in Vietnam. There has been no improvement in the last few years.

[338] Under the Bankruptcy Law,[351] a company is considered 'insolvent' if it fails to meet any of its payment obligations within three months from the due date.[352] A bankruptcy request can be submitted to a Vietnamese court after a company becomes insolvent by: (i) unsecured or partly secured creditors, (ii) employees/trade unions, or (iii) the insolvent company itself. The Bankruptcy Law does not impose a time limit for the filing of the bankruptcy petition. At law, if the company fails to make a bankruptcy filing upon becoming aware that the company has become insolvent, it would be subject to a monetary fine ranging from VND1 m to VND3 m.[353] Furthermore, the Bankruptcy Law seems to suggest that the relevant directors would also be liable for any damage that is caused by their failure to make a bankruptcy filing.[354] However, it does not specify what type of damage the directors would be held liable for. We are not aware of any instances where these requirements have been enforced in practice. In part, because of the size of the potential fine and the lack of clarity under the law, most directors decide not to make the filing, notwithstanding the fact that a large number of companies in Vietnam are actually insolvent.

[339] A purchase of shares of a company that is in bankruptcy (i.e., the court has issued a decision to open bankruptcy procedures)[355] would be possible if: (i) the creditors have passed a resolution on the recovery of that company's business and on the sale of shares of the company, and (ii) such resolution is approved by the court.[356] A purchase of assets in this case is also possible.[357] These are very complex and time-consuming deals that should only be contemplated by a foreign investor if there is absolutely no alternative means of reaching its business goals.

[340] In addition to bankruptcy court proceedings, a company may undertake out-of-court liquidation. Once a company passes a resolution on voluntary liquidation of the company, it must: (i) within seven working days send such resolution to the licensing authorities and to all creditors, employees and people who have rights and obligations relating to the company; and (ii) liquidate all outstanding debts and contracts of the company.

[351] Law No. 51/2014/QH13 on Bankruptcy of the National Assembly dated 19 Jun. 2014 (***Bankruptcy Law***).
[352] Article 4.1 of the Bankruptcy Law.
[353] Article 67 of Decree 82/2020/ND-CP of the Government dated 15 Jul. 2020.
[354] Article 28.5 of the Bankruptcy Law.
[355] Article 42 of the Bankruptcy Law.
[356] Articles 88 and 92 of the Bankruptcy Law.
[357] Article 88 of the Bankruptcy Law.

[341] The licensing authorities will remove the company from the national enterprise registration database: (i) within 180 days after it receives the liquidation resolution (unless there is any objection from a third party); or (ii) within five working days after the licensing authorities receive a request to do so from the company upon full payment of all outstanding debts.[358]

11 DUE DILIGENCE ISSUES

11.1 Due Diligence: The Vietnam Context

[342] Legal due diligence in Vietnam tends to focus on:

(a) the ownership of the target company and the extent of the capital contributed by the owners;
(b) business activities carried out by the target company and potential foreign ownership limits applicable to the target; and whether the target company is required to undertake a pre-sale restructuring;
(c) corporate governance of the target company and share transfer restrictions;
(d) the necessary authorisation, permits, licences and structure to carry on the target company's current and planned business. Among numerous other things, the buyer should examine whether the company obtained proper approvals at the time of establishment or in connection with important subsequent events, such as an increase in capital or transfer of interests;
(e) if the target company is foreign-owned and has an investment registration certificate, particular attention should be paid to the debt structure of the company. Often, a significant portion of a foreign-owned company's funding is supplied in the form of shareholder loans, which the seller may wish the buyer to assume. These loans have to be registered with the SBV. If they have not been, foreign currency cannot be remitted to pay interest or principal on the loans;
(f) the title to factory buildings, land use rights or other assets. Companies have sometimes been formed with little documentation evidencing precisely what assets were transferred into the company by the Vietnamese shareholders. This problem is more acute if a Vietnamese shareholder carries on a related business on an adjoining property;
(g) the true value of the assets being bought;
(h) any understated liabilities that may affect the on-going business or the Vietnamese participants' ability to perform their commitments to the company,
(i) tax concerns are a particular problem as many companies are believed to keep more than one set of accounts. In addition, transfer pricing is rising steadily as an area of concern;
(j) the extent of, and approvals received for, related-party transactions.

[358] Article 208 of the Enterprise Law.

[343] There are a number of other issues that often need to be investigated, depending on the nature of the target company, such as: (i) ownership of buildings, or defects in proof of ownership of such buildings; (ii) licences and permits necessary for occupying and using the building; (iii) nature of contracts entered into with staff of the target company (e.g., employment contracts, service contracts, cooperation contracts, etc.) and implications thereof; (iv) maintenance of internal labour rules; (v) contracts or arrangements with key personnel; (vi) trademarks and other intellectual property rights; (vii) compliance with environmental protection regulations; (viii) material contracts and change of control, termination events under these contracts; (ix) anti-bribery and corruption compliance; and (x) litigation (though there is no searchable court registry in Vietnam).

11.2 Due Diligence: Publicly Available Information

[344] Some limited information about Vietnamese companies is now publicly available (though there is no guarantee that such information is up-to-date):

(a) Information about the date of incorporation, name and address of the company, business lines, capital structures, details of the legal representative, and the latest change of the enterprise registration certificate of the company.
(b) The enterprise code, address, name of the legal representative, registered business lines and public announcements of companies are also available.
(c) Information about the bank account, applicable taxes and business lines of a company can be obtained from the General Department of Tax (***GDT***) if one has been provided with the tax code, name, address of the company or identification number of the company's legal representative.
(d) The National Registration Authority for Secured Transactions provides details of secured transactions and the descriptions of the secured assets involved that have been registered with them.
(e) The National Office of Intellectual Property provides information about registered trademarks, industrial designs or patents, including the registration certificate and a description of the intellectual property involved.
(f) Public or listed companies also have to disclose certain information, which can be found on the online databases of the SSC, the VSD and the relevant stock exchange.

11.3 Due Diligence: Systemic Issues

[345] Among the problems likely to be encountered in legal due diligence in Vietnam are:

(a) Substantial reliance has to be placed on the documents provided by the target company. Legal due diligence is therefore difficult and drawn out, with certain risks having to be managed. A national business registration database is now in operation but in practice is not necessarily up-to-date. Some local people's committees have begun to provide relevant information on their websites.

(b) Many Vietnamese sellers are not familiar with due diligence processes, so the exercise can be more cumbersome and take longer than in other jurisdictions. Data rooms often contain limited information, and most of the information provided is in the Vietnamese language.

(c) A disinclination to reveal information. One of the requirements for buyers and their advisors is to coax information out of target company staff that are predisposed towards secrecy as a result of long-ingrained business habits. This is especially prevalent among governmental officials reared within institutions with cultures of secrecy.

(d) A developing and as yet inadequate system of laws which makes precise legal analysis difficult.

[346] Business due diligence is also troublesome. Many vendor business plans (when they exist at all) are of limited reliability, with assumptions that lack support. The quality of accounting records is also sometimes a problem, and this can compromise the quality of business forecasts.

[347] Depending on the buyer, the quality, depth and integrity of management are often reviewed closely. Obtaining reliable management information is often difficult without the support of the management itself. Private investigatory agencies are hard to find and often provide a service of questionable value.

11.4 Corruption

[348] Corruption remains a problem in Vietnam. In Transparency International's *Corruption Perceptions Index*, Vietnam ranks poorly (although its ranking has improved in recent years).[359] The current General Secretary of the Communist Party is committed to an anti-corruption campaign. In recent times, various State officials and owners, directors and executives of Vietnam's banks and companies (both State-owned companies and non-State-owned companies) have been arrested or convicted. For investors, it is critical to know as much as possible about the target company, its owners and directors, and their respective connections with State officials or businesses that are or may be under investigation in order to avoid becoming embroiled in an undesirable situation.

[349] Foreign investors need to bear their obligations in mind under applicable laws of extraterritorial application (e.g., Foreign Corrupt Practices Act, UK Bribery Act) and Vietnamese anti-bribery laws, which, despite general appearances, are both severe and sometimes enforced. On an ongoing basis, for both foreign and domestic compliance reasons, employees should be appropriately trained in how to do business without bribery.

[359] Available at: https://www.transparency.org/.

[350] Before investing in a Vietnamese target, investors should undertake thorough due diligence which covers, among other things, the target company's owners, business activities, reputation and relationships. In sensitive situations, a full analysis of the implications is only possible with extensive cross-checks.

(a) Criminal Code

[351] Any person who offers a bribe of VND2 000 000 (approximately USD85) or more commits a criminal offence.[360] To constitute a criminal offence, the person who offers a bribe (or uses an intermediary to offer a bribe) must do so with the intent of obtaining some direct or indirect benefit.

[352] The offence is believed to be the counterpart of the criminal offence of receiving bribes under Article 354 of the Criminal Code. This is defined as an act of a person who holds an official position or power and directly or indirectly receives money, assets or other 'material benefit'[361] or 'non-material benefit' 'with the intent of taking advantage of his/her official position or power in order to perform or refrain from performing certain acts for the benefit of, or as requested by, the person who offers the bribe'.

(b) Anti-Corruption Law

[353] The Anti-Corruption Law prohibits 'corrupt acts'.[362] The law contains a broad definition of 'corrupt acts': it includes 'taking bribes', 'abusing position and power to appropriate properties' and a wide variety of other actions 'for self-seeking interests'.

[354] Even more broadly:

> Organisations, agencies and office holders must not directly or indirectly receive gifts in any form from another organisation, agency or individual that is relevant to the tasks/matters they are performing/handling or tasks/matters under their respective management.[363]

11.5 Money-Laundering Regulations

[355] Vietnam has laws on anti-money laundering (AML).[364] Under the AML Law, reporting entities include (i) financial institutions entities that are licensed to

[360] Article 364 of the Criminal Code No. 100/2015/QH13 of the National Assembly dated 27 Nov. 2015, as amended by Law No. 12/2017/QH14 (the ***Criminal Code***).

[361] Which has a value of VND2 000 000 (approximately USD85) or more.

[362] Anti-Corruption Law No. 36/2018/QH14 of the National Assembly dated 20 Nov. 2018 (***Anti-Corruption Law***).

[363] Article 22.2 of the Anti-Corruption Law. This applies to both the public and the private sector.

[364] Law No. 14/2022/QH15 on AML of the National Assembly dated 15 Nov. 2022 (***AML Law***) and Decree 19/2023/ND-CP of the Government dated 28 Apr. on implementation of the AML Law (***Decree 19***).

undertake some banking, financial, securities or insurance, and (ii) certain non-financial persons which conduct such activities as gaming businesses, real estate businesses, accountant services, notary services, legal services or precious stones or metals. They are required to take anti-money laundering measures and comply with other statutory obligations (e.g., reporting obligations).[365] For instance, a reporting entity must:

(a) conduct customer due diligence or know your customer procedures and assess money-laundering risks;[366]
(b) set up internal regulations on AML;[367]
(c) report large transactions or suspicious transactions;[368]
(d) apply provisional measures to delay or freeze transactions.[369]

[356] A breach of AML regulations could result in disciplinary actions, administrative fines, criminal and/or civil liabilities.

11.6 Environmental Laws

[357] Under the Environment Law,[370] investment projects are categorised into high-risk, medium-risk, low-risk and zero-risk groups (groups I to IV). The environmental risk level determines the environmental licensing requirements that apply to a project, i.e., whether a project is subject to (A) a preliminary assessment of environmental impact; (B) a full environmental impact assessment in the feasibility study phase; (C) an environmental permit; or (D) environmental registration.[371]

[358] If the project of a target company is a group I project, the target company must have done a preliminary assessment of environmental impact at the pre-feasibility or application for approval-in-principle phase.[372]

[359] If the project is a group I or II project (unless it is a small or medium-scale and capacity project involved in production, business and services), the target company must have prepared an environmental impact assessment report, which would include:[373]

365 Article 4 of the AML Law.

366 Section 1 Ch. II of the AML Law.

367 Article 24 of the AML Law.

368 Articles 25–37 of the AML Law.

369 Section 1 Ch. II of the AML Law.

370 Law No. 72/2020/QH14 on Environment Protection of the National Assembly dated 17 Nov. 2020 (***Environment Law***).

371 Articles 29 to 49 of the Environment Law.

372 Article 29 of the Environment Law; Decree 54/2021/ND-CP of the Government dated 21 May 2021 on preliminary assessment of environmental impact.

373 Article 32 of the Environment Law.

(a) specifications of the project;
(b) conformity of the project with the laws and relevant planning;
(c) operational technology of the project;
(d) measures to minimise any negative effects on the environment;
(e) an undertaking to apply environmental protection measures during construction and operation; and
(f) opinions of the local people's committee and the community where the project is carried out.

[360] An environmental impact assessment report will be evaluated and approved by the MONRE, line ministries, or the provincial people's committees, depending on which category the project falls in.[374]

[361] A project of group I, II or III requires a construction permit if there are emissions and/or waste discharges requiring treatment during operations,[375] and if the project generates waste but does not reach the level for which an environmental permit is required, the investor of the project needs to have an environmental registration.[376]

[362] If the target is required to obtain an environmental permit, it would have to submit an application to the competent authority, which is either the MONRE, the line ministries, or the provincial or district people's committee. An environmental permit, having a term of seven to ten years (i.e., renewable), allows the target company to discharge waste into the environment, manage waste, and import scrap from abroad as raw production materials, in accordance with the requirements and conditions on environmental protection as prescribed by laws.[377]

[363] If the target company has to do an environmental registration, this would be filed at the commune-level people's committee. It would include general information about the project; type of production or business, technology, capacity, raw materials, fuel and chemicals used; the volume of wastes; measures to treat and collect wastes; and other environmental commitments.[378]

[364] In the past, enforcement tended to be weak. However, a 2016 case involving mass fish death in central Vietnam as a result of a toxic discharge by a steel factory demonstrated that this is changing. The owner of the factory, in this case, agreed to pay USD500 m in compensation. Indeed, there are substantial potential liabilities for a buyer of a plant that does not meet the required standards:

(a) Article 602 of the Civil Code and the relevant provisions of the Environment Law require a person causing environmental pollution to compensate for damage where required by law, whether or not such person is at fault.

[374] Articles 34–36 of the Environment Law.
[375] Article 39 of the Environment Law.
[376] Article 49 of the Environment Law.
[377] Articles 3.8, 40 and 41 of the Environment Law.
[378] Article 49 of the Environment Law.

(b) Under Article 584.1 of the Civil Code, an organisation may have to compensate for damage if it is in breach of the regulations on environmental protection and thereby causes damage.
(c) Under Article 601.2 of the Civil Code, an owner of 'a source of extreme danger'[379] must compensate for damage caused by the source of extreme danger even if the owner is not at fault.

[365] Depending on the situation, criminal liabilities are also possible. Under the Criminal Code, these could be applicable to companies as well as individuals.

11.7 Product Safety Laws

[366] While there is no specific product liability legislation in Vietnam, the Civil Code, the Commercial Law,[380] the Law on the Protection of Consumer Interests,[381] and the Law on the Quality of Goods and Products[382] all contain provisions that are applicable to product liability issues. The legislation is sufficiently broadly drafted to impose a form of strict liability on organisations that manufacture, import or trade in goods that are found to be defective. Breach of the legislation may result in the imposition of fines and administrative sanctions and claims for loss and damage.

[367] The regulations also include an obligation for manufacturers and importers of goods to institute a product recall in appropriate circumstances, although the regulations provide no guidance on the circumstances in which a product recall should be carried out or how it should be done.

11.8 Intellectual Property Rights

[368] The Law on Intellectual Property[383] and its implementing regulations provide a legal basis for registration, protection and enforcement of intellectual property rights. The same type of intellectual property due diligence is carried out regardless of whether there is a share sale or an asset sale. In general, due diligence includes:

---

379 Sources of extreme danger are defined to include motorised means of transport, power transmission systems, operating industrial plants, weapons, explosives, inflammable substances, toxic substances, radioactive substances, dangerous animals and other sources of extreme danger stipulated by law. Article 601.1 of the Civil Code.

380 Law No. 36/2005/QH11 on Commerce of the National Assembly dated 14 Jun. 2005 (***Commercial Law***).

381 Law No. 59/2010/QH12 on Protection of Consumers' Interests of the National Assembly dated 17 Nov. 2010, which will be amended from 1 Jul. 2024.

382 Law No. 05/2007/QH12 on the Quality of Goods and Products of the National Assembly dated 21 Nov. 2007.

383 Law No. 50/2005/QH11 on Intellectual Property of the National Assembly dated 29 Nov. 2005 (as amended on 1 Jan. 2010, 1 Nov. 2019 and 1 Jan. 2023).

(a) a check of the validity of intellectual property registrations. Law firms can request trademark, design and patent searches of the official database of the National Office of Intellectual Property of Vietnam. There is a public database, but it is incomplete and not always available or reliable;
(b) reviews to determine whether the products of the target company tend to infringe on third-party intellectual property rights;
(c) scrutiny of licence agreements to assess contractual protections and obligations, and to determine whether they have been registered.

[369] It is advisable to examine whether a trademark has been used in Vietnam because it can be subject to a cancellation action for non-use if it is not used within five years prior to the date of a request for its cancellation based on non-use.

[370] Additionally, if the acquisition is in the pharmaceutical, health, beauty product or food sectors, product registrations with the relevant ministry are normally checked for validity.

[371] If intellectual property has been created by the target company, the buyer should confirm whether the target company's contracts with its employees provide that the employees do not own any intellectual property rights and are not entitled to any statutory royalties. Employees may retain moral rights, including the right of attribution and the right to have the integrity of the work protected. It is unclear whether moral rights can be waived, but it is prudent to ask the employee to sign a waiver of any moral rights.

11.9 Distributors and Agents

[372] There are no regulations specifically governing distributorship arrangements. Vietnamese regulations governing the sale of goods and civil contractual relationships would apply between sellers, distributors and users of products. These include: (i) the Commercial Law, (ii) the Civil Code, and (iii) laws relating to such matters as competition, trademark licences, trade promotion, advertising and product quality.

[373] Under Vietnamese law, a distributorship arrangement may be categorised in one of two ways:

(a) It could be a sale and purchase contract containing a distribution element. The local distributor would purchase goods from the principal for resale in Vietnam under certain standards imposed by the principal. Under this arrangement, the distributor will own the goods before selling them to customers.
(b) Alternatively, it could be a sales agency contract. The local distributor would act as a sales agent for the principal to sell goods in Vietnam. Under this arrangement, the principal will remain the owner of the goods until sold.

[374] If a distribution agreement is deemed to be an agency arrangement, then, unless otherwise agreed, (i) it can only be terminated after a reasonable period of time and not less than sixty days from the date of service of a termination notice; and (ii) if the principal serves a notice of termination on the agent, the agent is entitled upon termination to one month's agency remuneration for each year that the agent has acted for the principal.[384]

11.10 Valuation Issues

[375] Historically, the common approach of Vietnamese sellers was to determine the sales price of a business by valuing the assets of the business, often without appropriately valuing intangible assets (such as access to a customer base or trademarks or brands), or any off-balance-sheet exposures. This approach appears to be in decline. However, in the valuation of SOEs, the value of real estate holdings is often an important focus both for the State and for potential buyers.[385]

[376] In practice, many buyers now use earnings multiples, reflecting company and market-specific risk factors, to value targets in Vietnam. Comparable businesses and transactions (if they exist), growth potential, the quality of management, and the possibility of improving performance are often the main factors influencing the multiple that is selected. There is often a substantial amount of judgement that is needed due to the lack of comparable data and due to the general unreliability of data of all sorts, including financial results. This has sometimes led to valuations that, with hindsight, appear optimistic.

[377] Some buyers use discounted cash flow as the main valuation tool. The problem is that the business planning of many Vietnamese companies still often does not generate much trust. Furthermore, sellers have tended to be slow to realise the benefits of engaging financial advisors to improve confidence in business plans, though, again, this is gradually changing.

[378] In general, the price expectations of sellers are often unrealistically high, and this has contributed to the failure of numerous negotiations.

11.11 Change of Control Clauses

[379] Change of control clauses are relatively rare in Vietnamese contracts, and they do not tend to affect many negotiations. Such clauses exist in some offshore contracts, including bank documentation, if the target company has entered into

384 Article 177 of the Commercial Law.

385 There are detailed regulations on how valuation companies have to value State assets. But that does not preclude buyers from looking at potential values after potential re-zoning. For example, a strategic investor in the privatisation of the national textile company, Vinatex, was a real estate development company known as Vingroup. Press commentary suggested that the focus of the investment might not be textiles as much as the company's real estate holdings.

such contracts. This is the case, for example, in the context of infrastructure companies using offshore project finance, where bank consent to ownership changes is usually required.[386]

[380] Change of control clauses also exist in certain onshore contracts, particularly loan contracts. Where they exist, they are expected to be enforceable. Sometimes, they have legal origins, as in production-sharing contracts used for offshore oil and gas exploration, where changes in control clauses are contemplated in the model contracts.[387]

11.12 Due Diligence of a Public Company and Insider Trading Rules

[381] The Securities Law prohibits the use of inside information to purchase or trade in shares of public companies. Failure to comply with the insider trading rules may result in a fine.[388]

[382] The broad definition of inside information[389] may include certain information obtained by a potential buyer in the course of due diligence into a public company. Therefore, theoretically, if an investment by a buyer in a public company is predicated on the use of inside information relating to the target company obtained by the buyer in the course of due diligence, the investment might be subject to insider trading restrictions under the Securities Law.

[383] Buyers tend to try to mitigate insider trading exposure when investing in a public company through one or more of the following:

(a) They can require representations from the target company or the seller (i) that all information provided to the buyer in the course of the buyer's due diligence has been disclosed to the public in accordance with the Securities Law, and (ii) that any undisclosed information which has been provided to the buyer would not have any effect on the target company's share price.
(b) They can obtain an undertaking from the target company that it will not make any claims on the grounds of insider trading restrictions under the securities regulations and will indemnify the buyer against any actions taken by third parties on the grounds of insider trading restrictions.

---

[386] The bigger issue in these infrastructure company ownership transfers has tended to be the extent of the need for government consents, given the various acknowledgements that various government entities may have provided to the original owners or lenders. Each situation depends on the documents and how they were drafted.

[387] *See*, for example, the model contract issued pursuant to Decree 33 of the Government dated 22 Apr. 2013.

[388] Articles 12.2 and 132 of the Securities Law.

[389] 'Inside information' is defined in Art. 4.44 of the Securities Law as information relating to a public company which has not been disclosed and which, if disclosed, may materially affect the share price of the public company.

(c) The buyer may obtain some limited comfort from receiving governmental approvals if the purchase is of a nature that such approval is required.[390]
(d) The buyer may create internal records evidencing that its decision to acquire shares in a public company is not based on inside information of the public company.

11.13 State Secrets

[384] Potential buyers should also be aware of the laws on State secrets. The Law on Protection of State Secrets[391] prohibits any illegal collection, disclosure, appropriation, sale and purchase, and destruction of State secrets (unless approval has been obtained from a competent authority).[392]

[385] Although a buyer would not normally come into contact with information classified as State secrets in practice, it has to be aware of the potential for information to be withheld during its due diligence and consider the representations and warranties that are required in order to provide protection in respect of unknown, withheld information. If a buyer does in fact obtain such information, it would need to obtain approvals from a competent State authority in charge of the relevant State secret before collecting, storing, using, processing, transferring and/or sharing it.

[386] State secrets are defined under the Law on Protection of State Secrets[393] as:

> Information, in any form, carrying important contents as determined by the head of the competent authority in accordance with the Law on Protection of State Secrets, which has not been publicised and the disclosure of which may cause harm to the interests of the nation or the people of the Socialist Republic of Vietnam.

Under the Law on Protection of State Secrets, State secrets are divided into three levels: (i) top secrets, (ii) extreme secrets, and (iii) secrets:

(a) Top Secrets.[394] State secrets classified as 'top secret' are those related to politics, national defence and security, cryptography and foreign affairs whose divulgence or loss can cause *exceptionally grave damage* to the national interests.
(b) Extreme Secrets.[395] State secrets classified as 'extreme secret' are those related to politics, national defence and security, cryptography, constitution

[390] In practice, in certain high visibility projects, special comfort on the point has sometimes been obtained from the SSC.

[391] Law on Protection of State Secrets No. 29/2018/QH14 of National Assembly dated 15 Nov. 2018 (***Law on Protection of State Secrets***).

[392] Article 5 of the Law on Protection of State Secrets.

[393] Article 2.1 of Law on Protection of State Secrets.

[394] Article 8.1 of the Law on Protection of State Secrets.

[395] Article 8.2 of the Law on Protection of State Secrets.

formulation, legislation, judiciary, foreign affairs, economy, resources and the environment, science and technology, education and training, culture, sport, information and communications, healthcare, population, labour and social affairs, organisational structure and official affairs, inspection, supervision, handling of violations, settlement of complaints and denunciations, anti-corruption and state audit whose divulgence or loss can cause extremely grave damage to the national interests.

(c) Secrets.[396] State secrets classified as 'confidential' are those related to politics, national defence and security, cryptography, constitution formulation, legislation, judiciary, foreign affairs, economy, resources and the environment, science and technology, education and training, culture, sports, information and communications, healthcare, population, labour and social affairs, organisational structure and official affairs, inspection, supervision, handling of violations, settlement of complaints and denunciation, anti-corruption and state audit whose divulgence or loss can cause grave damage to the national interest.

[387] The Prime Minister promulgates lists of secrets based on proposals of the entity responsible for the supervision of each area.[397] In the banking sector, the list of State secrets is promulgated under Decision 2182/QD-TTg of the Prime Minister dated 21 December 2020 including:

(i) **Top Secrets**: (1) undisclosed plans and schemes for issuance of new currency; (2) undisclosed projects, proposals, and results of recall and exchange of old currency; and (3) undisclosed plans, projects and proposals for designing and making printing plates of specimen currency.

(ii) **Extreme Secrets**: (1) designs of currency (i.e., bank notes) and valuable papers that have been approved by competent authorities, but have not been made public; files of currency and valuable security designs approved by competent authorities; prints, engravings, films, moulds, stampings of currency and valuable security; files for creating prints, engravings, films, moulds, stampings of currency and valuable security; test printing, test casting, and stamping samples of currency and valuable security approved by competent authorities; (2) currency printing ink formulas; technical specifications of currency printing inks that have not been made public; technical specifications used in the process of making prints, moulds, stampings of currency and valuable security issued by the SBV; regulations on quality, technical specifications in the process of printing, minting, stamping currency and valuable security issued by the SBV; and (3) security locks, technical specifications, special anti-counterfeiting features of currency and valuable security issued by the SBV.

[396] Article 8.3 of the Law on Protection of State Secrets.

[397] For instance, the Prime Minister issued Decision 1441/QD-TTg on 23 Sep. 2020 to promulgate the list of State secrets in investment and statistics sector, Decision 531/QD-TTg on 19 May 2023 to promulgate the list of State secrets in education and training sector, and Decision 1451/QD-TTg on 24 Sep. 2020 to promulgate the list of State secrets in employment and social sector.

(iii) **Secrets**: (1) the SBV's plans for the future implementation of the national monetary policy; (2) the SBV's total money supply data which are not made available to the public; (3) in-country stockpiles of physical gold as part of the State foreign exchange reserves; (4) self-examination reports on vault safety operations of affiliates of the SBV: reports on internal audit, reports on supervisory results of the SBV regarding vault safety operations and management of the State foreign exchange reserves: the SBV's inspection records on the State foreign exchange reserve management activities; (5) absolute data on total revenue, total expenditure, cash surplus and deficit within the SBV; (6) amount of money printed, minted and issued; (7) documents regulating the letters and numbers of currencies and valuable security instruments; (8) money transfer plans, money orders, schedules, telegrams of transportation of money, precious assets or security instruments; (9) data on dispatch, receipt, inventory of cash, precious assets, valuable security instruments which are released by the Reserves, e.g., data on dispatch, receipt of destroyed money, plans to destroy money; (10) plans to purchase money printing paper, money printing ink, money stamping moulds, money stamping ingots; documents on dispensing of series alphabets for money printing activities; (11) design documents, locations, plans and proposals for the security of money printing and minting establishments: central currency stockpiles, regional currency stockpiles, currency processing and storage centres of the SBV; (12) absolute data on the amounts of counterfeit money seized through the banking and State Treasury system; (13) reports of inspection of money printing and minting establishments by the SBV; (14) financial statements of the National Currency Printing Factory; (15) reports on results of fulfilment of the tasks of asset safety supervision of the SBV at the Central Money Vaults or Stockpiles; (16) statements of financial supervision of the National Currency Printing Factory by the SBV; (17) annual and five-year business plans, financial plans of the National Currency Printing Factory; (18) charts of bookkeeping accounts, balance sheets of the SBV; (19) results of the SBV's annual rating of credit institutions which have not been made available to the public; (20) information, documents, data about insolvency, risk of insolvency or illiquidity, risk of illiquidity of commercial banks, cooperative banks, people's credit funds; (21) various information and documents on the special control of cooperative banks and people's credit funds; (22) undisclosed information about the restructuring and disposal of bad debts of poor-ranked commercial banks, cooperative banks and people's credit funds in accordance with the law; (23) schemes or projects on restructuring and disposing of bad debts of credit institutions that have not yet been made public; written requests of the SBV for opinions of ministries, sectoral administrations and opinions of ministries, sectoral administrations pertaining to the restructuring and disposal of bad debts of credit institutions: reports of the SBV to the Government, the Prime Minister and competent authorities on the contents of the projects on restructuring and disposing of bad debts of credit institutions; (24) amounts, maturity periods of special loans, maturity date extension in credit institutions' loan applications which have not yet been made public; amounts, terms of special loans, or extension of special loan due dates, which have not been publicly disclosed; and (25) SBV interactions with competent anti-money laundering authorities and prevention and control of terrorism financing.

11.14 Personal Data Projection

[388] The Government of Vietnam has issued a decree on personal data protection, Decree 13/2023/ND-CP (***Decree 13***), which took effect from 1 July 2023.

[389] Decree 13 applies to (i) Vietnamese organisations and individuals, including those operating overseas; and (ii) foreign organisations and individuals in Vietnam, or participating in or relating to personal data processing activities in Vietnam.[398]

[390] Decree 13 includes the concepts of 'Data Controller' and 'Data Processor':

- Data Controller is the organisation or individual that decides the purpose of, and means for, personal data processing.[399]
- Data Processor is the organisation or individual that processes data on behalf of the Data Controller on a contractual basis.[400]
- Data Controller-Processor is the organisation or individual that does both the activities set out above.[401]

[391] Generally, the Data Controller has more obligations towards the data subjects and the authorities, including obtaining consent and performing the data subjects' requests relating to their personal data, recording and archiving system logs of data processing, and is liable to the data subjects for any damage caused by the data processing activities.

[392] Decree 13 requires the Data Controller or Data Processor to conduct an impact assessment and maintain the assessment dossier from the time it starts personal data processing. It must also submit the dossier to the personal data protection agency for approval within sixty days after starting data processing. The authority will review and can request an update of the dossier if it is not yet compliant.[402]

[393] Personal data of Vietnamese citizens offshore are permitted to be transferred offshore, provided that the party that transfers personal data of Vietnamese citizens offshore must conduct an impact assessment and maintain the assessment dossier from the time it starts data processing. It must also submit the dossier to the personal data protection agency within sixty days after starting data processing.

[398] Article 1 of Decree 13.
[399] Article 2.9 of Decree 13.
[400] Article 2.10 of Decree 13.
[401] Article 2.11 of Decree 13.
[402] Article 24 of Decree 13.

Similar to the case of general processing of personal data, the authority will review and can request an update of the dossier.[403]

11.15 Representations and Warranties

[394] As a result of the difficulties inherent in obtaining accurate and trustworthy information, the best due diligence involves regular meetings between all strands of the due diligence team in order for each work-stream to know the findings of the others in real-time. This enables further work to be done by each strand with a fuller picture and makes it easier for suspicions or concerns to be followed up or eliminated promptly.

[395] Contractual representations and warranties come a poor second to due diligence in Vietnam but are relatively well-accepted.

[396] While Vietnamese law honours the principle of liability for breach of contractual provisions, there are important caveats, including the following:

(a) the measure of damage is restricted to 'actual direct loss' plus lost profits.[404] It is possible to provide for limited 'penalties' or liquidated punitive damages, but it is doubtful whether the combination can exceed the loss and the lost profits;
(b) the difficulties of being confident in the correct outcome of any dispute that may arise; and
(c) Vietnamese law does not have a concept of indemnification as provided under English law. Unless the concept is specifically spelt out in contractual documentation, a court in Vietnam is likely to ignore an indemnification and apply its normal liability principles. If the concept is specifically spelt out in contractual documentation, the court may determine the extent to which the agreed principles are consistent with such liability principles and may enforce the indemnity to that extent.

11.16 Practical Advice

[397] The limitations of due diligence in Vietnam and the prevalence of substandard record-keeping often make it difficult to fully assess contingent and off-balance-sheet liabilities, including exposure related to tax, licensing, employment and environmental risks.

[398] Accordingly, one of the key difficulties in Vietnamese acquisitions is reaching an agreement on the allocation of risk among the parties, which in turn impacts

403 Article 25 of Decree 13.
404 Article 302 of the Commercial Law.

negotiations on price, representations and warranties, covenants and indemnities, often in a fundamental way. For example, it is not uncommon for a seller to refuse to represent that the target company has obtained the necessary licences to carry out its business in Vietnam.

[399] Seasoned advisers acting for both the buyer and seller can mitigate this obstacle, as there is a market practice in Vietnam on some of these issues.

[400] For issues where there is not a settled market practice, well-qualified advisers familiar with the market, who can provide informed, balanced and practical advice, can help clients avoid taking overly cautious or overly optimistic approaches, both of which can kill a deal or lead to future problems if the deal goes through.

12 LAW AND DISPUTE RESOLUTION

12.1 Governing Law

[401] In light of the inherent risks contained in Vietnamese law, a threshold question for any foreign acquirer is whether the law of a foreign jurisdiction can be chosen to govern transaction documents.

[402] Parties to a commercial contract involving a 'foreign element' are permitted to apply a foreign law, but only to the extent that such law is not contrary to the basic principles of Vietnamese law.[405] The contours of the basic principles of Vietnamese law are unclear. This can make it difficult to be sure about the effectiveness of a contractual choice of foreign law. Indeed, this issue has occasionally been a reason advanced by Vietnamese courts for not enforcing foreign arbitral awards in Vietnam, though it is not clear whether other reasons also existed or would also have been found in such cases for the lack of enforcement.

[403] Vietnamese law does not specifically prohibit Vietnamese State-owned companies from entering into contracts governed by foreign law. However, in practice, governmental agencies and State-owned entities tend to be suspicious of foreign law. They tend to resist entering into foreign law-governed contracts. Indeed, there is often a lack of understanding of the difference between the law of contract and the law governing the operations of an entity in Vietnam. All that being said, many examples exist of contracts with such agencies and entities that are governed by foreign law.

[404] It used to be possible, though it was usually difficult, to obtain a legal opinion from the Ministry of Justice on the legality and enforceability of foreign law-governed contracts. Under 2015 regulations, such official legal opinions will now be limited to contracts signed by the State and the Government.[406]

[405] Article 5.2 of the Commercial Law and Arts 670 and 683 of the Civil Code.

[406] Decree No. 51/2015/ND-CP on issuance of legal opinions of the Government dated 26 May 2015.

12.2 Contracts Governed by Vietnamese Law

[405] Many transactions are documented under Vietnamese law. Even if the main governing law is foreign, some documents, such as shareholders' agreements, are usually governed by Vietnamese law because they deal with the operation of a Vietnamese company. There are various general issues and risks that could arise from using Vietnamese law as the governing law of a contract.

(a) Predictability

[406] Vietnamese law lacks predictability. Vietnamese law is not well developed, consistent or clear, nor does it have a meaningful system of binding case law[407] or other interpretative aids of binding precedential value. Vietnamese law changes frequently, which does not help to increase the stability and predictability of the law.

[407] Vietnamese law is also subject to broad interpretation. Different officials, lawyers and courts can have contrasting views of the legality or validity of a particular regulation. The ultimate arbiter in Vietnam of the interpretation of the law is, as a matter of practice, often the ministry or agency responsible for administering the relevant law or regulation. Even then, it is possible that different agencies and officials will have different views as to the interpretation of Vietnamese law and the basis on which it should be implemented. This results in Vietnamese law providing more fertile ground for disputes between the parties, as well as potentially increasing the scope of disputes and the time taken to resolve them.

[408] By contrast, many foreign law systems that are more developed than Vietnamese law are based on a system of precedent that dates back many centuries. In considering questions of breach of contract, the parties are able to refer to a body of law in which it is likely that a similar issue will have arisen in similar circumstances. This should serve to reduce the number of potential areas of dispute as well as the time taken to resolve the dispute.

(b) Unfamiliar System of Law

[409] Vietnamese courts and arbitration forums are unpredictable. Consequently, foreign parties to contracts tend to try to provide for dispute resolution by arbitration in a foreign jurisdiction. Since Vietnam has acceded to the 1958 New York Convention on the enforcement of foreign arbitration awards, foreign arbitration awards are, at least in theory, enforceable in Vietnam.

[410] While reference to foreign arbitration is likely to make for a more predictable outcome in any dispute, the arbitrators are unlikely to be familiar with Vietnamese law. This, together with the fact that Vietnamese law is subject to widely different

[407] Published court precedents are recognised as a source of laws to govern civil relations in Vietnam pursuant to Resolution No. 3/2015/NQ-HDTP of the Justice Council of the Supreme People's Court dated 28 Oct. 2015 on the selection, publication and application of court precedents as replaced by Resolution No. 04/2019/NQ-HDTP dated 18 Jun. 2019 on the same matter. However, the published precedent system (available at https://anle.toaan.gov.vn/webcenter/portal/anle/anle, last accessed on 1 Mar. 2023) remains meagre in light of both the quantity and quality of the selected precedents.

interpretations, is likely to result in lengthier proceedings in the event that a dispute is referred to arbitration than would be the case if the law of a more sophisticated jurisdiction were to be chosen as the governing law.

(c) Confidence in the Certainty of the Contractual Bargain

[411] The principle that English public policy requires full freedom of contract and that contracts should be sacred and enforceable has at least 140 years of provenance.[408] By contrast, the Vietnamese Civil Code provides room for courts to impose obligations of good faith or reasonableness. Furthermore, rules of interpretation contrast with those of English law. For example, acts may be interpreted in accordance with the 'customs of the place where the transaction is established'.[409] And if one party introduces into a contract a term that is detrimental to the other party, such contract term is to be interpreted in a manner favourable to the other party.[410]

[412] Parties to some contracts have sought to mitigate the problems of Vietnamese law as a governing law by including foreign law as a 'gap filler'. However, the position is probably not much improved by a 'gap filling' provision as it would not be clear in what circumstances the foreign law would apply. First, Vietnamese law is generally sufficiently ambiguous and vague to enable the Vietnamese party to argue in many circumstances that Vietnamese law is not silent on a particular issue. Second, there is a principle of Vietnamese law to the effect that in the absence of any law on a particular matter, other provisions of Vietnamese law can be referred to by analogy.[411] Third, foreign law could not be applied if it was not consistent with the 'basic principles' of Vietnamese law.[412]

12.3 Dispute Resolution: Vietnamese Courts

[413] Litigation and arbitration are not rare in Vietnam. The courts of Vietnam are not generally regarded as reliable by foreign businesses. Some of the reasons for this are as follows:

---

408 *See* the words of *Sir George Jessel in Printing and Numerical Registering Co. v. Sampson* [1875] 5 LR 19 Eq 462.

409 Article 404.3 of the Civil Code.

410 Article 404.6 of the Civil Code.

411 Article 5 of the Civil Code.

412 Under the Civil Code, the application of relevant law must not be contrary to the principles set out in Art. 3, which includes the following principles:

(i) equal treatment between persons;
(ii) freely and voluntarily entering into commitments and/or agreements which do not violate regulations of law and are not contrary to social order;
(iii) goodwill and honesty in establishing, exercising/ fulfilling, or terminating civil rights and/or obligations;
(iv) not infringing national interests, public interests, lawful rights and interests of other persons in establishing, exercising/ fulfilling, or terminating civil rights and/or obligations;
(v) liability for failure to fulfil or the incorrect fulfilment of civil obligations.

(a) Vietnamese laws are often not clear and well drafted.
(b) Commentators often take the view that the Vietnamese courts tend to be biased in favour of Vietnamese parties, particularly powerful State-owned companies.
(c) The courts in Vietnam do not operate with a system of binding precedent, so there is no legal requirement regarding the uniformity of decision-making.
(d) The ability of Vietnamese judges to read and understand materials and documents in foreign languages is believed to be limited.
(e) Although, in theory, a dispute should be subject to two hearings (first instance and appeal), in practice, a dispute may be subject to various hearings and re-hearings due to the fact that many authorities have the right to request a rehearing.

[414] Given the weaknesses of the court system in Vietnam, it is difficult to provide general recommendations for court litigation in Vietnam. A foreign party to a court litigation proceeding in Vietnam should take into account the possible weaknesses of the court system when developing its litigation strategy. Reaching an out-of-court settlement is often better than court proceedings.

[415] There is no Vietnamese law explicitly addressing the issue of sovereign or other immunity of State-owned companies. Vietnamese law does not make a clear distinction between public/governmental acts and private/commercial acts.[413] Furthermore, Vietnamese jurisprudence is not well-developed, and it is possible that courts may imply or create immunities that have not been legislated. Companies entering into contractual relationships with State authorities or State-owned companies should include clear waivers of sovereign immunity. Article 100.1(b) of the Civil Code seems to recognise the waiver of sovereign immunity by a State agency.

12.4 Dispute Resolution: Vietnamese Arbitration

[416] The Arbitration Law[414] has attempted to bring arbitration in Vietnam closer to international standards. It has adopted new provisions relating to the scope of the disputes eligible for arbitration, injunctive relief, increased power and autonomy of tribunals and the ability of foreigners to act as arbitrators and operate arbitration centres in Vietnam. However, the rules of Vietnamese arbitration remain less developed than foreign arbitrations. For instance, the arbitration rules

[413] Under international law, a State and its property are immune from suit and execution of judgment. There are currently two doctrines concerning sovereign immunity. Western countries adopt the restrictive doctrine of immunity whereby a State and its property are explicitly immune from suit and execution of judgment only to the extent of public acts but not commercial acts. Some former communist countries adopted the doctrine of absolute sovereign immunity, pursuant to which a State and its property are explicitly immune from suit and execution of judgment. It is unclear which doctrine Vietnam follows.

[414] Law No. 54/2010/QH12 on Commercial Arbitration of the National Assembly dated 17 Jul. 2010 (***Arbitration Law***).

of the Vietnam International Arbitration Centre (***VIAC***), the most notable arbitration centre in the country, contain no procedures for the joinder of parties, or procedures for early dismissal of the claim.[415] The list of arbitrators in Vietnam arbitration is more limited than that of other regional arbitration centres, such as the Singapore International Arbitration Centre or the Hong Kong International Centre. Many arbitrators may not be well-trained or well-versed in complicated commercial issues, and they may be susceptible to inducements. Although the position is improving, there are uncertainties surrounding the enforceability of certain arbitration awards, and these will continue to hamper the growth of arbitration in Vietnam.[416] The law gives Vietnamese courts significant discretion to reject awards that might otherwise be legitimate. For example, decisions of arbitral tribunals must not be contrary to fundamental principles of Vietnamese law.[417] The court may also reject an arbitral award if it decides that the tribunal had no authority to consider the case or that there was no valid arbitration agreement.[418]

[417] The VIAC, which consists of both local and foreign arbitrators and is the busiest arbitration centre, handled about 292 cases in 2022.[419]This is probably in part because arbitration is not well accepted by businesses and in part because there are problems enforcing arbitral awards.

12.5 Dispute Resolution: Foreign Courts

[418] In some cases, even if the parties' legal relations must be governed by the laws of Vietnam, their disputes may be resolved in a judicial forum outside the country. However, foreign court judgments can only be enforced in Vietnam if the judgment has been recognised by an authorised Vietnamese court. A Vietnamese

---

415 *See* https://www.viac.vn/en/rules-of-arbitration.html.

416 There have been reports that the number of arbitral awards being set aside has decreased over the years 2005–2020 (information provided in the conference themed 'Summary of 20 Years of Implementation of the 1958 New York Convention on Recognition and Enforcement of Foreign Arbitral Awards', held by the Ministry of Justice in Hanoi on 21 Nov. 2014, and the online conference themed 'Arbitrators and Arbitral Proceedings', held by the ADR Vietnam Chamber LLC on 15 May 2020). Awards being set aside have tended to be high-value awards (as compared with those awards being enforced) and the reasoning given in such set-aside decisions remains controversial (for example, Decision No. 11/2019/QD-PQTT of the Hanoi People's Court dated 14 Nov. 2019 on setting aside Final Award VIAC 24/14 in relation to the dispute between Vinh Son Song Hinh Hydropower JSC and the consortium of Hydrochina Huadong Engineering Corporation and the China Railway 18th Bureau Group – available at: https://congbobanan.toaan.gov.vn/2ta428188t1cvn/chi-tiet-ban-an (in Vietnamese) (last accessed on 1 Mar. 2023)).

417 Article 68.1 of the Arbitration Law. In March 2014, in Resolution 1/2014 implementing the Law on Commercial Arbitration, the Supreme Court for the first time gave some limited guidance by referring to certain principles contained in the Civil Code, the Commercial Law and the Law on Commercial Arbitration as examples of fundamental principles of Vietnamese law.

418 In recent case (available at https://congbobanan.toaan.gov.vn/2ta139515t1cvn/chi-tiet-ban-an), the court in Hanoi rejected a decision of the VIAC on the ground that a debt acknowledgement signed by a debtor, which included an arbitration provision, did not constitute a valid arbitration agreement between the parties.

419 VIAC report in 2022 (available at https://www.viac.vn/en/statistics/2022-stattistic-s41.html).

court will only recognise: (i) judgments of a country which, together with Vietnam, has signed or acceded to international treaties on the matter (but Vietnam has not signed any such treaties), and (ii) judgments which are permitted to be recognised by Vietnamese law, such as those permitted on the basis of reciprocity.[420] Vietnam has signed bilateral treaties on reciprocal enforcement of court judgments with a few countries, most of which are from the former communist block: Russia, Cuba, Czech Republic, Slovakia, Hungary, Bulgaria, Poland, China, Laos and North Korea. The notable additions to this list are France and Taiwan.

[419] The orders and judgments of the courts of most developed jurisdictions would therefore not be recognised in Vietnam. As such, judgments of foreign courts are largely unenforceable against assets in Vietnam. Foreign court proceedings may, however, still be desirable if the Vietnamese party has assets outside Vietnam.

12.6 Dispute Resolution: Foreign Arbitration

[420] As a result of the difficulties inherent in litigation or arbitration in Vietnam, and the potential problems with a foreign court judgment, many cross-border transactions refer disputes to offshore arbitration.[421] A properly drafted arbitration clause will improve the prospects of enforcement.

[421] A foreign arbitral award is not enforced directly in Vietnam but must be recognised and held enforceable by a Vietnamese court.[422] In principle, a Vietnamese court may recognise and enforce an award rendered by an arbitration panel of 'a country that is a party to a relevant international treaty of which Vietnam is a participant or a signatory', i.e., the New York Convention on the Recognition and Enforcement of Foreign Arbitral Awards (the New York Convention), to which Vietnam has acceded. In addition, recognition and enforcement of foreign arbitral awards are also permitted on the basis of reciprocity, without participation in an international treaty.

[422] The recognition procedures for enforcement of a foreign arbitral award are set out in the Civil Procedure Code. Consistent with the principles of the New York Convention, Vietnamese law provides that a court is not to review and reconsider the merits of the arbitral award but only to check compliance with the provisions of the legal proceedings.[423]

---

[420] Article 423 of the Civil Procedure Code dated 23 Nov. 2015 (the ***Civil Procedure Code***). The resolution of the Justice Council of the Supreme People's Court guiding the implementation of certain provisions of the Civil Procedure Code on recognition and enforcement of foreign awards at first-instance courts remains in the draft form circulated for public opinion in mid-2019.

[421] Under Art. 14 of the Investment Law, disputes between domestic investors must be submitted to Vietnamese courts or Vietnamese arbitrations.

[422] Article 427.3 of the Civil Procedure Code.

[423] Article 438.4 of the Civil Procedure Code.

[423] An application for recognition and enforcement of a foreign arbitral award may be rejected by a Vietnamese court if the respondent can adduce evidence to prove that:

(a) the parties lacked the capacity to sign the arbitration agreement in accordance with the law applicable to each party;
(b) the arbitration agreement is invalid under applicable law;
(c) the respondent did not receive sufficient notice of the appointment of arbitrators or the arbitration proceedings or for other legitimate reasons the respondent could not exercise its rights in the proceedings;
(d) the foreign arbitration award was made where no settlement was requested or was made beyond the request of the parties;
(e) the composition of the arbitration body and/or the arbitration proceedings was not in accordance with the arbitration agreement of the parties or applicable law;
(f) the award is not yet binding on the parties; or
(g) the award has been overruled or suspended by the competent authorities of the countries where the award was made or whose law was the governing law.

[424] A Vietnamese court may also reject an application for recognition and enforcement of a foreign arbitral award if it decides that the dispute should not be resolved by way of arbitration under Vietnamese law or that the recognition and enforcement of the award are contrary to 'basic principles of Vietnamese law'. As a result of these factors, the recognition and enforcement of foreign arbitration awards is considered in practice to be unpredictable.[424]

12.7 Dispute Resolution: Investor-State Arbitration

[425] Vietnam has signed sixty-seven bilateral investment treaties, is party to twenty-seven treaties with investment provisions, and is a member of nineteen free trade agreements. Some of these include provisions for Investor-State dispute settlement. There have been some disputes between investors and the Vietnamese government.

[424] On 17 Jan. 2023, the High Court in Hanoi refused to recognise a SIAC arbitration award in relation to the dispute between Global Payment SE/UTC Investment Co. Ltd. and VMG Media arising from a share purchase agreement on the following grounds: (i) the arbitration award was contrary to fundamental principles of the laws of Vietnam (namely, it is unfair for VMG that the hearing was held before the Supreme People's Court having the final decision in respect of operations of EPay, the target company); (ii) the application of the Misrepresentation Act of Singapore, and disregarding Vietnamese law, are against fundamental principles of the laws of Vietnam; and (iii) if the enforcement of the SIAC award were allowed, then VMG's real properties in Vietnam would be realised for enforcement, against the exclusive jurisdiction of Vietnamese courts (available at Công bố bản án, quyết định của tòa án (toaan.gov.vn)).

12.8 Strategic Considerations

[426] Aside from the usual considerations involved in deciding whether to commence litigation or arbitration that apply in any jurisdiction (expenditure of time, money, etc.), it is important to consider the potential for collateral damage to the foreign investor that could occur following the commencement of an action against a Vietnamese party, whether the foreign investor ultimately wins or loses the action.

[427] The risk of collateral damage, which could take the form of reputational damage in Vietnam, difficulty in operating other businesses in Vietnam, or difficulty exiting other investments, can increase if the foreign investor has or plans to have substantial investments in Vietnam, or if the Vietnamese counterparty has strong connections in the government or influence on the media.

[428] Reputational damage can also be a two-way street, and many Vietnamese companies would seek to avoid a public and potentially embarrassing legal dispute with a foreign investor.

[429] These considerations should be kept in mind during negotiations and the drafting of legal documents. The goal, first and foremost, of the draftsman should be to decrease the chances of a dispute, and second, to provide as many practical options as possible for the foreign investor if and when a dispute does arise.

13 MERGER CONTROL

13.1 Background

[430] The Competition Law[425] and its implementing regulations[426] (the ***Competition Regulations***) form the basis of a competition law framework in Vietnam. But this framework remains largely untested in Vietnam.[427] And many key issues and definitions are vague.

[431] The current competition authority is the Viet Nam Competition Commission (***VCC***) under the MOIT. The VCC is in charge of antitrust matters, including economic concentration control and anti-competitive acts.[428]

425 Law No. 23/2018/QH14 of the National Assembly dated 12 Jun. 2018 (***Competition Law***).

426 The implementing decrees issued to date include Decree 35/2020/ND-CP of the Government dated 24 Mar. 2020 implementing the Competition Law (***Decree 35***); and Decree 75/2019/ND-CP of the Government dated 26 Sep. 2019 on handling violations of the Competition Law (***Decree 75***).

427 There have been some merger investigations in recent years. The VCCA has looked at the acquisition of Metro Cash & Carry Vietnam by TCC Holding, the acquisition of Big C, a Casino-owned supermarket chain, by Central Group, the merger of Lixil and American Standard, the acquisition of Sanofi products by Boehringer, and the merger of Uber into Grab.

428 Decree 03/2023/ND-CP of the Government dated 10 Feb. 2023 on functions, duties, powers and organisational structure of Viet Nam Competition Commission.

[432] The Competition Law prohibits an economic concentration that causes or is likely to cause a significant restraint of competition in the Vietnamese market.[429] Whether a merger notification filing to the VCC is required for a proposed 'economic concentration' depends on:

(a) whether the proposed transaction is an 'economic concentration'; and
(b) whether the proposed transaction meets one of the filing thresholds set out in Decree 35.[430]

13.2 Economic Concentrations

[433] An economic concentration is broadly defined to include:

(a) mergers of enterprises;
(b) consolidations of enterprises;
(c) acquisitions of an enterprise;
(d) joint ventures between enterprises; and
(e) other forms of economic concentration, including the acquisition of shares in an existing enterprise, if such acquisition gives the buyer the right to 'control' the target company.[431]

[434] A buyer would have 'control' of a target company if it:[432]

(a) acquires more than 50% of the charter capital or the voting shares of the target; or
(b) acquires the right to own or use more than 50% of the assets of the entire business or one business line of the target; or
(c) has the right to make decisions regarding any of the following in respect of the target:
    (i) (either direct or indirect) appointment or removal of a majority of or all of the directors, the chair of the members' council or the CEO or the general director;
    (ii) amendment of the charter; or
    (iii) important business activities, those being the organisation of the business operation, business lines, the geographic scope of the operations, the mode of doing business, adjustment of the scope of the business and the business lines and the forms and methods of raising, allocating and utilising capital.

429 Article 30 of the Competition Law.
430 Article 33 of the Competition Law and Art. 13 of Decree 35.
431 Article 29 of the Competition Law.
432 Article 2.1 of Decree 35.

13.3 Filing Thresholds

[435] An economic concentration will need to be notified to the VCC if it meets one of the thresholds set out in the table below:

Sectors	*Turnover*	*Assets*	*Transaction Value*	*Combined Market Shares*
Insurance	VND10 t	VND15 t	VND3 t	20% or more in the relevant market in Vietnam
Securities	VND3 t	VND15 t	VND3 t	20% or more in the relevant market in Vietnam
Credit institutions	20% or more of the total turnover of credit institutions in Vietnam	20% or more of the total assets of credit institutions in Vietnam	20% or more of the total charter capital of credit institutions in Vietnam	20% or more in the relevant market in Vietnam
All other sectors	VND3 t	VND3 t	VND1 t	20% or more in the relevant market in Vietnam

For purposes of the above:

(a) The 'turnover' and 'assets' thresholds are calculated on a group-wide basis.[433]
(b) The law is silent with regard to whether only the market shares of the direct parties to the transaction (as opposed to the market shares calculated on a group-wide basis) would be taken into account when it comes to determining whether the market share threshold test has been met. However, in precedent filings under the old competition law,[434] the Vietnam Competition and Consumer Protection Authority (VCCA), the predecessor of VCC, took into

[433] A group is defined as 'a group of enterprises which are under common control by one or more of the enterprises in the group or which are under the common management'.

[434] Law No. 27/2004/QH11 of the National Assembly dated 3 Dec. 2004, which has been replaced by the Competition Law since 1 Jul. 2019.

account the market share on a group-wide basis, and the same approach may be expected to continue to apply.

(c) The law is unclear on whether the turnover and assets thresholds will apply separately to each party to the economic concentration or on a combined basis to all the parties to the economic concentration.

(d) The VCC may launch an investigation into a transaction if it receives a complaint, or there are signs that the transaction (despite not being notifiable) has the effect of significantly restraining competition within three years of the closing date of the transaction.

13.4 Relevant Market

[436] Prior to any notification filing to the VCC (if the transaction constitutes an 'economic concentration' and meets one of the notification thresholds), the parties would need to define the 'relevant market'.

[437] A relevant product market is the market of all products and/or services which are regarded as interchangeable or could be substituted for each other in terms of characteristics, purposes of use, and price.[435] Decree 35 contains more specific factors to consider in determining the scope of a relevant product market.[436]

[438] A relevant geographical market comprises a specific geographical area that is:[437]

(a) significantly different from neighbouring areas;
(b) with goods or services that may be substituted for each other; and
(c) defined by homogeneous conditions of competition.

[439] In determining whether a geographical area is significantly different from neighbouring areas, the VCC would take into account a number of factors, including whether enterprises in surrounding areas are able to participate in the distribution network, costs and duration of transport and various other barriers to market entry.[438] The conditions for competition would be regarded as homogeneous (and significantly different from neighbouring areas) if one of the specifically enumerated geographical barriers to market entry was found to exist, such as retail price increases of 10% or more as a result of the costs and duration of transport.[439]

---

435 Article 9.1 of the Competition Law.

436 Article 4 of Decree 35. The Competition Regulations allow for the application of other criteria, economic analysis and various tests if these measures are insufficient to determine the relevant product market. *See*, for example, Arts 4.5, 4.6, 5 and 6 of Decree 35.

437 Article 7.1 of Decree 35.

438 Article 7.2 of Decree 35.

439 Articles 7.3 and 8 of Decree 35.

13.5 Merger Filings

[440] The parties to an economic concentration must themselves determine whether or not a filing threshold is met. If it is, they must notify the VCC. If the parties determine that a filing threshold has been exceeded and notify the VCC, the VCC will evaluate whether the parties' declaration is correct and whether the concentration is permitted.

[441] If the parties determine that none of the filing thresholds has been exceeded and proceed with the economic concentration without notifying the VCC, and the VCC later determines that the parties were wrong, these parties may be exposed to an administrative fine of up to 5% of the total turnover of each participating party in the relevant market in Vietnam in the fiscal year prior to the year of closing the transaction. Other administrative sanctions may also be applied, such as the confiscation of proceeds from the breach of the competition law and revocation of the business certificate or licence of the parties. If the parties fail to notify the VCC of the transaction and the VCC later determines that the transaction should be prohibited, the parties might be exposed to additional administrative fines, and they could be ordered to unwind the transaction.

13.6 Procedures and Scope of Substantive Review

[442] A merger notification file must be submitted to the VCC prior to the completion of the economic concentration. A notification file includes, with respect to all enterprises participating in the economic concentration:[440]

(a) a prescribed form describing the proposed transaction and the details of the parties;
(b) a draft economic concentration agreement or term sheet, a memorandum of understanding or a draft summary of the terms of the proposed transaction;
(c) copies of the incorporation certificates or equivalent documents of each party;
(d) audited financial statements of each party for the two consecutive fiscal years preceding the economic concentration;
(e) a list of the affiliates of each party;
(f) a list of the products and services provided by each party;
(g) the market share data or a report of each party for the two consecutive years preceding the economic concentration;
(h) a plan for addressing any possible restraint of competition as a result of the economic concentration; and
(i) a report on the assessment of the positive impact of the economic concentration.

[443] Within seven working days, the VCC will check the completeness of the file and issue a written confirmation on whether the notification file is complete or not.

[440] This means that both the buyer and seller would have to make the filing.

If it is not, the VCC will request the parties to provide additional information or documents, and the parties will have thirty days to respond.[441]

[444] Thirty days from the date the VCC issues a written confirmation on the completeness of the file, the VCC will conduct the preliminary review. If the transaction does not pass the test in the preliminary review, the VCC will continue with an official review, which may take up to 150 days.

13.7 Jurisdiction

[445] The Competition Regulations apply to 'relevant domestic and foreign agencies, organisations and individuals.'[442] This is a new provision in the Competition Law, which aims to cover foreign-to-foreign transactions that cause or may cause a restraint to competition in Vietnam.[443]

[446] There is some uncertainty because the language is so vague, but the VCCA/VCC takes the view that the asset and turnover tests apply both to the buyer and the target on a combined basis and also to the buyer or the target individually:

(a) However, the Competition Law does not apply in a situation where there would be no impact on competition, and none is likely. So, if the target has no assets or turnover in Vietnam, it is possible that the parties can decide that no notification is necessary. The parties would have to determine in light of all the facts if they can avail themselves of this position.
(b) If the target meets the asset or turnover test, but the buyer has nothing in Vietnam, reliance on Article 1 of the Competition Law may be harder (though there may be room for discussion in specific contexts and this may evolve in practice).

13.8 Penalties

[447] The penalties for violations of Vietnam's merger control regime are as follows:

(a) Failure to notify: 1%–5% of the total turnover of each party (in the year prior to the infringement) for failure to notify the VCC if required.[444] Additional measures that might be applied are:
  (i) withdrawal of business licences of the parties;
  (ii) confiscation of exhibits and facilities used for committing the violation;
  (iii) confiscation of proceeds of the violation; and

[441] If the parties fail to satisfy the request of the VCC, the VCC will return the notification file to the parties and the parties will need to re-submit a new file to the VCC.
[442] Article 2.3 of the Competition Law.
[443] Article 1 of the Competition Law.
[444] Article 14 of Decree 75.

(iv) other necessary measures to remedy the effects of the violation.

(b) Prohibited economic concentration: Each party to the economic concentration is liable for a fine of up to 5% of total turnover in the preceding financial year.[445] In addition:
   (i) the parties could be ordered to unwind the transaction; and/or
   (ii) the parties could be placed under the control of the competent authorities for a certain period of time so that they can monitor the sale and purchase prices of goods or other conditions set out in the transaction agreements.[446]

13.9 Criminal Penalties

[448] Under the Criminal Code, it is a criminal offence to:[447]

(a) enter into an agreement to prevent another enterprise from participating in the market or developing its business;
(b) enter into an agreement to eliminate another enterprise not being a party to such agreement from the market;
(c) enter into an agreement to limit competition when the parties to such agreement have a total combined market share of 30% or more, including:
   (i) an agreement to directly or indirectly fix prices of goods or services;
   (ii) an agreement to allocate the market and the supply of goods or services;
   (iii) an agreement to restrict or control the volume or quantity of goods or services to the market;
   (iv) an agreement to restrict technological development or investment;
   (v) an agreement to impose tying conditions on sales.

[449] Under the current Criminal Code, companies can be prosecuted for criminal acts.

14 TAXATION

14.1 Asset Acquisitions

[450] In asset acquisitions, the seller and the buyer face a number of tax obligations.[448] As a result of these obligations, as well as non-tax and licensing issues,

[445] Articles 10–13 of Decree 75.

[446] *Ibid.*

[447] Article 217 of the Criminal Code.

[448] The tax rules applicable to acquisitions are characterised by uncertainties and by a lack of interpretative guidance. Both the substantive provisions of Vietnam's tax law and the interpretation and application of such provisions by the Vietnam tax authorities may be subject to more rapid and

most acquisitions in Vietnam occur in the form of share purchases. However, asset acquisitions still occur in some cases. These are primarily where:

(a) the existing share ownership is difficult to confirm or there are too many shareholders;
(b) there are potential liabilities in the existing company and the buyer believes that an asset purchase provides some protection;
(c) the buyer wants the ability to rebase the asset value for tax depreciation purposes;
(d) the target contains some businesses that the buyer does not want, and such unwanted businesses cannot be easily carved out;
(e) the buyer only wants to acquire a part of the target business; and
(f) the buyer cannot get financing for a share acquisition.[449]

[451] A foreign investor wishing to acquire assets of a Vietnamese entity must establish an entity to hold such assets in Vietnam. If the foreign investor already has an existing Vietnamese entity, the business licence of that entity may need to be amended to allow for expanded activities following the purchase of assets.

14.2 Tax Consequences of Asset Acquisitions

(a) Taxes

[452] A seller will be subject to a 20% CIT on any profit from the sale of assets.[450] The purchase price can be agreed by the two parties, though in transactions between related parties, the price must comply with the transfer pricing rules.[451]

[453] The buyer of the assets also has to pay value added tax (***VAT***), the rate of which depends on the nature of the assets in question but will normally range from 5% to 10% of the sale price.[452] There are no specific rules in Vietnam related to the transfer of a going concern and favourable VAT treatment. Official Letter 4445/TCT-DNL dated 14 November 2018 states that where the transferred assets and working capital are attributable to the taxpayer's supply of exempt services, the transfer of such assets and working capital is exempt from VAT. Where the fixed

---

unpredictable change than in a more developed jurisdiction. Furthermore, the interpretation and application of the tax rules in practice rests substantially with local tax inspectors.

449 *See* Section 'Acquisition Financing'.

450 Article 10 of the CIT Law.

451 Decree 132/2020/ND-CP of the Government dated 5 Nov. 2020 on tax management in respect of companies having transactions involving related parties (***Decree 132***). Under Decree 132, acceptable methodologies for determination of arm's length prices are similar to those adopted by Organisation for Economic Co-operation and Development for multinational companies and tax administrations, i.e., comparable uncontrolled price, resale price, cost plus, profit split and comparable profits method.

452 During the period from 1 Jul. 2023 to 31 Dec. 2023, VAT rate for certain goods/services is reduced from 10% to 8%. Decree 44/2023/ND-CP of the Government dated 30 Jun. 2023.

assets, tools, equipment, leasehold improvement costs and rental prepayments are not attributable to the taxpayer's supply of exempt services, the transfer of these items is subject to VAT at 10%. Further, transfer proceeds that are not the consideration for the supply of goods or services do not have to be reported for VAT purposes. This implies that in an asset transfer of a business where the value of fixed/ current assets and the value of goodwill are segregated, the value of goodwill is not subject to VAT.

[454] The VAT can probably be offset against any output VAT assessed on the future business of the buyer, but this will need to be verified based on specific circumstances applicable to the buyer, as it depends on the buyer having business activities of its own.[453]

[455] Buyers of assets (but not shares) must also pay registration taxes (up to VND500 m (approximately USD21 277))[454] for certain assets, such as:

(i) land and housing: 0.5%;[455]
(ii) ships and boats: 1%;
(iii) motorcycles: 1%–5%; and
(iv) automobiles: 2%, except for (A) automobiles with less than ten seats which are 10%, (B) pick-up trucks and vans with less than six seats and carrying capacity of fewer than 950 kilograms which are 6%, and (C) battery-electric cars which are from 0% to 5% for five years from 1 March 2023 for the first registration and 2% thereafter.

(b) Accrued Liabilities

[456] In principle, the buyer should not inherit any accrued tax liabilities of the seller company. However, the tax laws do not specifically protect a buyer of all the assets of a business from a claim by the tax authorities for back taxes of the target company. On the contrary, there are provisions of the law that, by analogy, might authorise the tax authorities to pursue the buyer as the successor in the interest of the business.[456] Even if these specific provisions of the law are not applicable or are not applied by analogy, the authorities could assert substance over form and make a claim against the buyer as the new owner of the assets/business. Given the vagueness of tax principles as applied to corporate acquisitions, any buyer-friendly acquisition contract should be specific about the liability of the seller for past tax liabilities (or, if practical in the circumstances, make a tax clearance certificate a condition precedent to closing). It should also contain representations that the

[453] Law on VAT of the National Assembly dated 3 Jun. 2008, as amended on 1 Jan. 2014, 1 Jan. 2015 and 1 Jul. 2016 (the ***VAT Law***).

[454] Article 8 of Decree No. 10/2022/ND-CP dated 15 Jan. 2022 governing registration fees (***Decree 10***).

[455] This would not apply to a 'transfer' of land use rights if the 'transfer' is in effect a return by the seller to the State followed by a new lease to the buyer.

[456] *See* Art. 68 of the Law on Tax Management of the National Assembly dated 13 Jun. 2019. This applies to mergers, consolidations and conversions. In asset acquisitions in other countries courts often impose liability on the buyer where the transaction essentially amounts to a consolidation or merger of the seller and buyer (based, for example, on the buyer's retention of the same management, personnel, location and business obligations, and the seller dissolves soon after the sale)

seller will use the sale proceeds to pay such taxes. If possible, such warranties should be backed up by indemnities.

(c) Carry-Forward Losses

[457] Carry-forward losses are generally not transferable on a sale of assets. Tax incentives remain with the seller of the assets and will normally be lost to the buyer.

(d) Depreciation

[458] The purchase price can be depreciated for tax purposes. The original cost of the fixed assets is the actual price paid plus any directly related expenses. The tax rules allow the cost of assets to be written off against profits by means of tax depreciation where certain conditions are met. Depreciation of both new and used fixed assets is calculated based on the historical cost and useful life of the fixed assets within the time frame in the regulations (which a business can determine for itself).[457]

[459] A fixed asset for tax depreciation purposes is one that meets the following conditions:[458]

(i) there is a high degree of certainty that a future profit will be obtained from using the asset;
(ii) the useful life of such asset is at least one year; and
(iii) the value of such asset is at least VND30 000 000.

[460] The transaction must be supported by valid documents.

14.3 Share Acquisitions

(a) Tax on Transfer of Capital Contribution in an LLC

[461] Income, if any, from a transfer of capital in an LLC is taxable at the rate of 20%. The taxable income is the transfer price less the cost base. The transfer price should be evidenced by a sale and purchase agreement. The cost base consists of the acquisition cost and transactional expenses:[459]

(i) the acquisition cost is, in general terms, the value of the transferor's capital at the time of contribution to the company being transferred; and

---

457 The depreciation time frame for plant and equipment is from two to thirty years, depending on the type of equipment. The depreciation time frame for intangible assets is from two to twenty years. Like goodwill, patents and know-how are not considered as intangible fixed assets for tax purposes and may only be amortised.

458 Article 3.1 of Circular 45/2013/TT-BTC of the MOF dated 25 Apr. 2013 (as amended on 28 Nov. 2016 and 26 May 2017) providing guidance on management, usage and depreciation of fixed assets.

459 Article 14 of Circular 78/2014/TT-BTC of the MOF dated 18 Jun. 2014 (as amended on 1 Sep. 2014, 15 Nov. 2014, 6 Aug. 2015, 1 Jul. 2016, 1 Sep. 2016 and 1 May 2018) providing guidelines on implementation of Decree 218 of the Government dated 26 Dec. 2013 guiding implementation of the CIT Law (***Circular 78***).

(ii) transactional expenses are the actual expenses incurred in relation to the transfer, as supported by legitimate invoices or other supporting documents. These may include legal expenses, levies, expenses relating to communications, negotiations, etc.

[462] If the capital being transferred is denominated in Vietnamese Dong, the transfer price and the cost base will be calculated in Vietnamese Dong. The exchange rate at the time of transfer will be used to determine the transfer price. The exchange rate at the time of the capital contribution will be used to determine the cost base. This may give rise to a material taxable gain due to exchange rate differences over time.

[463] If the seller is a foreign entity, the capital transfer tax must be withheld by the Vietnamese buyer, which is required to file a capital transfer tax return with the Vietnamese tax authorities. If the buyer is also a foreign entity, then the Vietnamese company in which the interest is acquired is responsible for the administration of the capital transfer tax.[460]

[464] The exception to the above rule is that if the seller is an individual and non-tax resident, they are only required to pay 0.1% of the transfer price.[461]

(b) Tax on Sale of Shares: Non-Public JSCs

[465] When selling its shares in a non-public JSC, a seller which is a legal entity will be subject to capital transfer tax in the same manner that would apply in case of transfer of capital in an LLC.

[466] However, if the seller is an individual (irrespective of whether they are a resident or non-resident), they are only required to pay 0.1% of the transfer price.[462]

(c) Tax on Sale of Shares: Public JSCs

[467] Under Official Letter No. 12501/BTC-CST of the MOF dated 20 September 2010, transfers of shares in public companies (as defined by the Securities Law) are subject to the tax applicable to transfers of securities. If the seller is a foreign entity, this tax is a 'deemed profits' tax equivalent to 0.1% of the value of the sale transaction.[463] No relief is allowed for transaction costs, and no allowance is taken for the cost of investments (in other words, the existence of actual profits is irrelevant).

[468] However, if the seller is a Vietnamese entity, then gains by that entity from the transfer of shares are taxed at 20%.

---

460 Article 14.2(c) of Circular 78.

461 Article 20 of Circular No. 111/2013/TT-BTC of the MOF dated 15 Aug. 2013 guiding the Law on Personal Income Tax and its amendments and Decree No. 65/2013/ND-CP of the Government dated 1 Oct. 2013, as amended on 1 Sep. 2014, 15 Nov. 2014, 30 Jul. 2015, and 1 May 2018) (***Circular 111***).

462 Articles 11.2 and 20 of Circular 111. Under Art. 2.4(b) of Circular 111, income of individuals from the sales of shares in non-public companies is considered to be income of the sales of 'securities'.

463 Article 11.3(g) of Decree 218/2013/ND-CP of the Government dated 26 Dec. 2013 (as amended on 15 Nov. 2014, 1 Jan. 2015, 1 Feb. 2018, 7 May 2018 and 1 Jun. 2021) implementing the CIT Law (***Decree 218***).

[469] If the seller is an individual (irrespective of whether they are a resident or non-resident), they are only required to pay 0.1% of the transfer price.[464]

[470] The tax payable by a foreign seller is withheld and paid to the State either: (i) by the securities company if there is a sale of listed shares, or (ii) by the commercial bank where the foreign investor has opened its IICA.

(d) Tax Loss Carry-Forward Rights

[471] Tax losses of a company can be carried forward for up to five years, starting from the year in which the losses are first incurred. Losses incurred by the target company prior to the transaction may continue to be offset against the taxable income of such company after the transaction. There are no specific shareholder continuity tests in Vietnam. Nor are there any consolidation rules.

14.4 Structuring

(a) Offshore Transactions

[472] Capital transfer tax clearly applies to first-tier investment transfers. The law is not entirely clear on if and how Vietnamese capital transfer tax would apply if a transfer does not involve the change of the investor in the Vietnamese company (i.e., the transaction is structured outside of Vietnam at the holding company level and above). However, the tax authorities are becoming more aggressive in their efforts to tax offshore transactions.

[473] A foreign company is required to pay capital transfer tax on taxable income derived in Vietnam (i.e., income sourced from Vietnam irrespective of where the income is paid). In particular, Article 3.3 of Decree 218[465] reads as follows:

> 3. Taxable incomes earned in Vietnam by foreign enterprises prescribed in Points c and d Clause 2 Article 2 of the Law on Corporate income tax are incomes sourced in Vietnam from the provision of services, provision and distribution of goods, grant of loans, payment for copyrights for Vietnamese entities or foreign entities doing business in Vietnam, or from the transfer of capital, projects of investment, right to contribute capital, right to participate in projects of investment, right to mineral exploration, extraction, and refinement of minerals, regardless of the location of carrying out business.

[474] There is no definition of what this means. Based on the above, simple indirect disposal of a Vietnam investment (via the disposal of the offshore intermediate

464 Articles 11.2 and 20 of Circular 111.

465 As amended by Decree 12/2015/ND-CP of the Government dated 12 Feb. 2015.

holding company) is now at risk of being caught for Vietnam capital tax purposes.[466]

[475] This was supported by an instruction from the General Department of Tax (***GDT***) to a provincial tax department to consider imposing CIT on a purchase by a Vietnamese buyer of all the shares of a Hong Kong company from a foreign seller. The Hong Kong company owned shares in a joint venture company in Vietnam. The GDT stated that the purchase price that the foreign seller received from the Vietnamese buyer for its shares in the Hong Kong company would be taxable income arising in Vietnam.[467]

[476] However, it can be argued that the capital gain is not derived in Vietnam if:

(i) the share transfer does not involve the target company and has no impact on the target company's ownership structure or registered name in Vietnam; and
(ii) there are no other Vietnamese parties involved in the transaction.

[477] It can be argued further the tax regulations fail to provide guidance on how to calculate the taxable gains and corresponding capital gains tax and how to declare and pay capital gains tax in case of indirect transfers:

(i) the wording in the CIT circular regarding the determination of taxable income for capital gains tax purposes still reflects a direct transfer of the Vietnam company and does not cater for indirect transfers;
(ii) the tax administration rules do not provide any mechanism for capital gains tax declaration if capital gains tax was determined to apply. There is only guidance in this regard for direct transfers. There is no payment or filing obligation specified for indirect transfers.

[478] That being said, there have been some high-profile examples of tax authorities asserting the taxability of offshore transactions.[468] These are particularly likely where a foreign partner has upset a powerful local partner by selling its ownership interest in a joint venture company through a sale of an offshore holding vehicle in order to avoid the Vietnamese partner's pre-emptive rights.

(b) Dividend Payments

[479] It may be possible for the seller to realise part of the value of its investment by means of a presale dividend. After-tax retained earnings can be freely distributed to a corporate investor (in or out of Vietnam) without paying further

---

466 The exact mechanism on taxation is not current available, e.g., who should file, when, tax calculation basis, tax rates etc.

467 *See also* Official Letter No. 2747/TCT-CS of the MOF dated 12 Jul. 2018 to Syngeta Vietnam and Official Letter No. 866/TCT-CS of the MOF dated 2 Mar. 2020 to GUYOMARC'H.

468 One example was the 2016 sale of the offshore company that owned the Big C Vietnam supermarket chain to Central Group of Thailand. The GDT collected tax from the Vietnamese subsidiary. The local authorities were instructed not to change the legal representative until the tax was paid. This was a high-profile case. It is likely that there are many transactions of which the tax authorities are not aware or, if aware, decide not to pursue because the regulations are not clear. We understand that there have recently been more filings in respect of offshore transfers.

Vietnamese tax.[469] In such circumstances, the dividend would reduce the proceeds of the sale and thus the gain on sale. Individuals, however, have to pay personal income tax at the rate of 5% for any dividend they receive.

[480] A remittance of dividends abroad can only be made after audited financial statements have been issued, the CIT declaration for the relevant financial year has been made, and a clearance from the tax office has been received.

(c) Acquisition Financing

[481] There is a withholding tax on interest of 5% for cross-border debt financing.[470] The tax treaty with France is one of the few with a tax exemption for interest on commercial loans.

[482] In principle, a company can deduct interest expenses against its income. However, there are some qualifications:

(i) in order for interest and related expenses to be deductible, foreign loans need to be registered with the SBV;
(ii) although there are no thin capitalisation rules, in practice, if the project is subject to the investment registration certificate, the licensing authorities may not issue licences to highly leveraged companies; and
(iii) the interest rate that can be deducted for tax purposes is capped at 1.5 times the basic interest rate announced by the SBV as of the date of the loan agreement; and
(iv) there are limits on the deductibility of loan interest to related parties.[471]

14.5 Remittance

[483] Dividends and profits can be remitted outside of Vietnam free of tax.

14.6 Registration Fee

[484] There are no registration fees on transfers of shares.

14.7 Consolidation

[485] There are no tax consolidation rules in Vietnam.

---

[469] Save that Art. 90.1(dd) of Circular 200/2014/TT-BTC of the MOF dated 22 Dec. 2014 (***Circular 200***) states that 'if preference shares are considered payable loans, the dividends to be paid for such preference shares would be deemed as loan interest'. There is a 5% withholding tax on loan interest.

[470] Please also refer to s. 8.1 'Acquisition Financing'.

[471] *See* Decree 132.

14.8 Tax Treaties

[486] To date, Vietnam has entered into approximately eighty double taxation agreements, with a number of others under negotiation.[472] Some of these double taxation agreements contain exemptions from capital gains taxes.

[487] In the event of a conflict between double taxation agreements and Vietnamese tax laws, the double taxation agreements will take precedence. The problem that arises in practice is that, according to the regulations,[473] tax exemptions are not automatic. Applications for a tax exemption must be submitted to the MOF along with relevant documents, all of which must be translated into Vietnamese and notarised. While waiting for MOF approval, which can take substantial time, foreign investors must pay any applicable taxes.

[488] General anti-avoidance provisions have been introduced into the law, and these often complicate the process of obtaining MOF approval for a tax exemption. Double taxation agreement entitlements will be denied where the main purpose of the arrangement is to obtain beneficial treatment under the terms of the double taxation agreement (treaty shopping) or where the recipient of the income is not the beneficial owner. The guidance dictates that a substance over form analysis is required for beneficial ownership and outlines the factors to be considered:[474]

(a) where the recipient is obligated to distribute more than 50% of the income to an entity in a third country within twelve months;
(b) where the recipient has little or no business activities (except for the ownership over the assets or rights to create the income);
(c) where the recipient has business activities, but its assets, business activities or employees do not correspond to its profit;
(d) where the recipient has little or no control over, or right to dispose of, or risk in relation to, the income received or assets or rights to create the income;
(e) back-to-back arrangements;
(f) where the recipient is resident in a country with a low tax rate (less than 10%) but not due to the reason of incentive investment; and
(g) where the recipient is an intermediary or agent.

14.9 Risks

[489] The buyer of an ownership interest in a company will acquire an interest in a company with certain tax liabilities.[475] As many companies are believed to keep

[472] Double taxation agreements between Vietnam and the United States, Algeria, Egypt, Kuwait and Macedonia have not yet been ratified.

[473] Circular 205/2013/TT-BTC of the MOF dated 24 Dec. 2013 guiding the implementation of double taxation agreements (***Circular 205***).

[474] Article 6 of Circular 205.

[475] Article 9.3 of Circular 78.

more than one set of books, it is advisable for the buyer to conduct tax due diligence before acquisition in order to understand the extent of the issue. If problems are uncovered, buyers need to develop a realistic plan for dealing with the risks.[476]

14.10 Transfer Pricing

[490] There are various situations where transactions will be considered as being between related parties. Under the wide-ranging definition of related parties, any direct or indirect engagement of one or more parties in the management, control of, contribution of capital to, or investment in another party may constitute an affiliate relationship amongst the parties involved. The threshold of control by capital contribution is 25%. The definition also extends to certain significant supplier, customer and funding relationships between otherwise unrelated parties.[477]

[491] If the tax authorities believe that the consideration paid for a transfer of capital is not consistent with the market price, they will fix the consideration based on documents obtained from an investigation using the following factors:

(a) comparable prices in other similar transfer contracts;
(b) the current and future profitability of the target;
(c) past capital transfer prices;
(d) the scope of the target's business;
(e) current and future tax incentives of the target.

[492] In order for a purchaser or seller to establish the reasonableness of the capital transfer price, it would be useful to have third-party valuation reports, offers from other potential buyers, an analysis from a professional consultant of such purchase offers, and minutes of the board of the seller explaining the reasoning for the acceptance of the price.

15 EMPLOYMENT CONSIDERATIONS

15.1 General

[493] Employment in Vietnam is regulated by the Labour Code[478] and its implementing regulations[479] (the ***Labour Regulations***). Vietnamese labour laws apply to both local Vietnamese and expatriates working in Vietnam. Most importantly,

[476] Liabilities may exist under numerous sets of laws other than the tax laws, including the accounting laws, securities laws and corporate laws, not to mention the Criminal Code.

[477] Article 5 of Decree 132.

[478] Law No. 45/2019/QH14 of the National Assembly dated 20 Nov. 2019 (***Labour Code***).

[479] Including Decree 145/2020/ND-CP of the Government dated 14 Dec. 2020 guiding the implementation of a number of provisions of the Labour Code on labour conditions and labour relationship (***Decree 145***) and Circular 10/2020/TT-BLDTBXHO of the Ministry of Labour, War Invalids and

while employers are encouraged to grant more favourable treatment to employees than is required by the law, it is not possible to contract out of the terms of the employment legislation.

[494] Vietnamese employment law is generally protective of employees and is drafted with the intention of providing strong employee rights. Employment tribunals have a tendency to find in favour of employees and are inclined to resolve the many and various ambiguities in the Labour Regulations in favour of employees. As a consequence, employment considerations require sensitive and careful handling.

15.2 Severance

[495] One potential liability for buyers of Vietnamese companies is the extent of accrued severance obligations. In the context of an acquisition of shares, the buyer should factor these contingent liabilities into its analysis of the seller's accounts and into the price it is willing to pay.

15.3 Asset Transfer

[496] The Labour Code suggests that the transfer of employees in the context of an asset's acquisition (the ***Asset Transfer***) must be implemented in accordance with a labour usage plan adopted by the employer after consulting with its trade union or other body representing the labour force if the jobs of multiple employees are impacted.[480]

[497] A transfer of employees in an asset deal from the seller to the buyer is not automatic. It would at least involve a change in the identity of the employer and may also involve a change in workplace or physical working conditions. Under the Labour Code, an employee's consent is necessary to amend a labour contract, and in the absence of such consent, the labour contract must continue to be performed on the existing terms (or be terminated by mutual agreement between the parties).[481] Accordingly, a buyer in an assets deal should assume that employees would have the right to object to a proposed transfer of their contracts.[482]

Social Affairs (the ***MOLISA***) dated 12 Nov. 2020 on guiding the implementation of a number of provisions of the Labour Code on labour contract, collective conciliation council and jobs or works having adverse effects on reproduction health.

480 Articles 43 and 44.2 of the Labour Code.

481 Article 33 of the Labour Code.

482 An official at the MOLISA has unofficially indicated that a new labour contract should be entered into in the case of an Asset Transfer. Although this view is not binding on the MOLISA, it does suggest that regulators could be open to an employee's objection to proposed amendments to a labour contract raised by such a transfer.

15.4 Share Transfer

[498] In the context of a share acquisition which results in a transition of control in the target company from the seller to the buyer (the ***Share Transfer***), the employees would remain employed by the target company. An employee may resign if he/she has any issue with such a change of control.

[499] The Labour Code requires that the employer must adopt a labour usage plan in case of 'division or separation, consolidation or merger; sale, lease out or conversion of enterprise type; or on the transfer of the ownership or the right to use assets of the enterprise or cooperative *which impacts on the jobs of many employees*'.[483] It is not clear what 'impact' in this clause means, i.e., whether all Share Transfers, or only those Share Transfers which result in the termination of labour, will have to prepare a labour usage plan. The interpretation of this requirement in practice remains to be seen.

15.5 Resignation and Re-employment

[500] The transfer of employees from the target company to the buyer in an Asset Transfer can occur through a resignation by each employee from their employment with the target company followed by re-employment by the buyer. Where an employee who has been employed for a period of one year or more resigns, they may claim a severance payment equal to one-half of one month's salary (and benefits, if any) for every year of service (excluding any period in which the employee has been covered under the unemployment scheme)[484] (the ***Severance Allowance***).[485] If this approach is followed, the seller should be asked to pay the Severance Allowance (if any), and the buyer will not have the overhang of such severance obligations in the future.

15.6 Redundancy and Re-employment

[501] The target company can unilaterally terminate the employment of each employee on the grounds of 'organisational restructuring' or 'technological changes' or 'economic reasons'.[486] The buyer could then offer re-employment to those employees that it wishes to retain.[487] An employee who has been working for the target company for a year or more and whose labour contract is terminated in this manner would be entitled to a job-loss allowance equal to one month's salary

483 Article 43.1 of the Labour Code.

484 Unemployment insurance has been mandatory for Vietnamese employees since Jan. 2009. However, foreign employees were not required to pay unemployment insurance; hence special attention is needed in case the target has foreign employees.

485 Article 8 of Decree 145.

486 Article 42 of the Labour Code.

487 Articles 42 and 47 of the Labour Code.

(and benefits, if any) for every year of service (excluding any period in which the employee has been covered under the unemployment scheme), subject to a minimum payment of two months' salary and benefits (the ***Redundancy Allowance***).[488]

[502] In addition to liability for the Redundancy Allowances or Severance Allowances, as the case may be, the target company may also be liable for:

(a) payment of salary in lieu of any accrued annual leave that has not been taken by an employee prior to termination;[489]
(b) payment of accrued but unpaid annual bonus (if any) pro rata up to the date of termination;[490]
(c) any other amounts payable under the terms of the labour contracts of the target company's employees or payable under applicable labour rules and policies; and/or
(d) other benefits under staff benefits packages such as various types of insurance, sick leave, annual staff trips, staff share schemes and staff loans at preferential interest rates.

15.7 Transfer on the Basis of a Tripartite Agreement (Without Resignation)

[503] A transfer of employment contracts can be effected through a tripartite agreement between the relevant employee, the target company and the buyer. In essence, a tripartite agreement would set out the procedures for an employment transfer in a binding agreement between all three parties. There are certain advantages for the buyer. A tripartite agreement might acknowledge that the Asset Transfer applies and that the employee's contract is transferred to the buyer and will continue to be performed by the buyer. It could also include a waiver or delay of payment of financial obligations incurred by the target company to the transferred employee (including any liability to pay severance or redundancy allowances at the time of the acquisition). In practice, this structure has been used by buyers and target companies to mitigate the risks of triggering financial obligations.[491]

[504] This structure could also take into consideration the continuity of service of the transferred employee in the sense that benefits that the transferred employee is

488 *Ibid.*

489 Under Art. 113.3 of the Labour Code, untaken annual leave that is not used as a result of a 'loss of job' or 'resignation' would have to be paid to an employee.

490 Under the Labour Regulations the applicability of this liability would be determined by the labour contract or collective labour agreement. *See*, for example, Arts 103 and 104 of the Labour Code. As a matter of practice, thirteenth month bonus schemes are standard in Vietnam.

491 Whilst there is nothing at law that would stop the transferred employee from reaching an agreement with the buyer and the target company on a waiver or delay of the payment of financial obligations incurred by the target company to the transferred employee, the enforceability of such agreement would be questionable should the transferred employee changes his or her mind, and a dispute arises and is brought to local labour court by the transferred employee.

entitled to under his/her existing employment contract and under the law (e.g., the entitlement to annual leave which, by law, may need to be increased every five years of service)[492] may be counted towards benefits he/she will be entitled to when working with the succeeding employer.

[505] The tripartite agreement structure assumes that the target company's employees are willing to be transferred to the buyer. If an employee does not wish to be transferred, the employee may either:

(a) resign and claim a Severance Allowance (if applicable); or
(b) insist upon remaining employed by the target company.

15.8 Other Issues

[506] Provided that a tripartite agreement is used to transfer the employment of each employee and accrued liabilities are transferred to the buyer, it is not necessary to execute new labour contracts. Nonetheless, a prudent buyer should execute new labour contracts with employees (or amendments if appropriate) which clearly set out the entitlements of the employee in respect of the period before the new labour contracts.

[507] If there is a collective labour agreement in effect, the transfer of employees would have to comply with the terms of this agreement.

16 ACCOUNTING

16.1 Accounting Standards

[508] Vietnamese laws do not require Vietnamese enterprises to apply International Financial Reporting Standards (***IFRS***). All Vietnamese enterprises (including foreign-invested enterprises) are required to comply with the Law on Accounting[493] and to apply Vietnam Accounting Standards (***VAS***). Generally, VAS is an adaptation of the IFRS and includes certain provisions similar to those in the IFRS. However, it has been estimated that it will be 2026 before IFRS will be fully integrated into VAS.[494] In practice, some foreign-invested companies simultaneously prepare IFRS accounting statements and books for reporting to their offshore parent companies.

[492] Article 114 of the Labour Code.

[493] Law on Accounting No. 88/2015/QH13 of the National Assembly dated 20 Nov. 2015.

[494] According to Decision No. 345/QD-BTC of the Ministry of Finance dated 16 Mar. 2020 ratifying the application of IFRS in Vietnam, the application of IFRS will be implemented in 3 phases: (i) preparation phase (2019–2021), (ii) pilot phase (2022–2025), and (iii) compulsory application of IFRS (after year 2025).

16.2 Valuation

[509] One of the challenges of acquisitions in Vietnam, particularly in an SOE equitisation context, is to determine the real value of a company. Two of the main differences between VAS and IFRS are the concepts of fair value and impairment. Items like accounts receivable, inventory and fixed assets are reported on the balance sheet at cost under VAS but at fair value under IFRS. In a downturn, fair value can be less than cost. Receivables are reported as what can be collected and inventory at the price at which sales can occur. Non-performing loans are reported differently under VAS than under IFRS. Non-performing loans are calculated under a formula under VAS, but in fact, they may be much higher under IFRS and the fair value concept.

[510] One common problem under VAS is the difficulty in re-evaluation of fixed assets due to the lack of an official system of valuation. This is compounded by a general lack of compliance with the accounting requirements in respect of depreciation rates. These problems create difficulty in the assessment of the real financial standing of a target company. Inadequate record-keeping and inadequate accounting practices in Vietnam, therefore, continue to pose obstacles to the acquisitions of Vietnamese companies.

16.3 Acquisition Accounting

[511] VAS contains concepts for acquisition accounting that are similar to provisions in the IFRS. Companies are not at liberty to adopt merger accounting.

[512] In a share-for-share acquisition (although rare in Vietnam), share premium value would have to be transferred to a share premium account.

[513] Assets are generally held at the cost recorded in the accounting books, not the fair value. Accordingly, any changes in the assets or liabilities resulting from the buyer's intention or events occurring after the acquisition would be dealt with as post-acquisition items.

[514] No provisioning for reorganisation or integration is required. Costs and expenses relevant to a reorganisation or integration are treated as post-acquisition items.

[515] VAS contains certain requirements that have to be satisfied in order to recognise an intangible asset. Intangible assets may be amortised over their useful lives, except that perpetual land use rights have an indefinite life. No impairment review is required. The value of a recognised intangible asset has to be more than VND10 m.

[516] Goodwill in a merger or acquisition can be amortised through the profit and loss account.

16.4 Consolidation

[517] The effective transaction date is defined as the 'date of success of a transaction' without any further guidance. In practice, the effective transaction date (for accounting purposes) would usually be the date of registration in the shareholder register (applicable to non-public JSCs), the share subscription date (applicable to UPCom) or the order acceptance date (applicable to listed companies). Upon the completion of all procedures for the transfer of the title of the relevant equity or assets to the buyer, the profit arising from the sale would be accounted into the seller's profit and loss accounts. Under VAS, such profit would be treated as 'financial income' in a share deal and as 'other income' in an asset deal.[495]

[518] A deferred payment obligation is treated as a liability when incurred. Contingent consideration is treated in the same manner as other contingent liabilities (off-balance sheet). Accordingly, any adjustment of its value will affect the profit and loss accounts rather than the goodwill figure.

17 FUTURE DEVELOPMENTS

17.1 Reform Generally

[519] Vietnam's economy has been buoyant despite global headwinds caused by the COVID-19 pandemic, the US-China trade war (of which Vietnam actually seems to be emerging as the winner) and a disagreement with China over the extent of its claims to the East Sea. It continues to promote various institutional reforms, governance reforms and legal revisions to keep growth at reasonable levels, including a restructuring of the State sector, a stronger clampdown on corruption and the issuance of amended laws on competition, investment, enterprises, securities and the environment.

17.2 Financial Sector Consolidation and New Law on Credit Institutions

[520] With a view to reducing the number of credit institutions and restructuring weak banks, the SBV is encouraging consolidation in the finance sector. This bank restructuring process began in 2011 and will continue in the coming years.

[521] In terms of regulations, the National Assembly of Vietnam is in the process of amending the Law on Credit Institutions. The amended Law on Credit Institutions is expected to deal with cross-ownership practices and the handling of bad debts.

[495] Under VAS, there is no separation between extraordinary items and exceptional items or between 'above the line' and 'below the line'.

17.3 Real Estate Transactions and New Relevant Laws

[522] In the last twelve months, Vietnam's real estate market has been soft, with sales down, capital scarce, and many projects slowing to a halt. The arrest of several real estate developers, such as Tan Hoang Minh, FLC and Van Thinh Phat, coupled with the Government's effort to revamp local corporate bond issuance practices, had a significant impact on the market. Many real estate companies have been struggling with liquidity and unable to pay back debts when refinancing was rendered impossible by the high lending rates and banks' reluctance to lend more money to real estate developers. Companies that raised capital from local bonds (which was one of the main channels for fundraising for real estate developers) are under pressure to repay bondholders, even before maturity. The lack of new projects available for sale has created more difficulties for real estate companies. These have forced real estate companies to obtain new capital by selling or exchanging equity or assets for debt settlement purposes. This also means that there will be more transactions in special situations in the coming months.

[523] Foreign investors might be poised to benefit from the current downturn. In addition, foreign companies moving from China to avoid risks related to US-China trade tensions are creating sizeable demand for industrial land all over the country. Industrial and logistics properties in Vietnam are the preferred asset choice for foreign investors, with the country growing into a new global manufacturing hub, while the office segment is also in demand.

[524] Vietnam's real estate market witnessed a number of deals during the 2022 – 2023 period, mostly with overseas buyers who can arrange capital sources to counter the credit crunch in the country. These included Keppel Corporation acquiring a 49% stake in two adjacent residential projects in Ho Chi Minh City from Vietnamese property developer Khang Dien for USD135.42 m; Gamuda Land acquiring the entire Uni Galaxy project in the southern province of Binh Duong from Becamex ITC, and LOGOS Vietnam Logistics Venture and Manulife Investment Management setting up a joint venture to acquire an 11-hectare, build-to-suit logistics asset in the greater Ho Chi Minh City area. Many other foreign investors are talking with local real estate developers about the sales of real estate assets.

[525] In 2022 and 2023, the Government has taken various measures and issued several regulations to reduce the pressure on real estate developers and enable them to access funding sources. These measures and regulations are more or less short term. The National Assembly are considering a suite of new laws with the view to address inherent issues in the real estate sector, including the Law on Land (amended), Law on Real Estate Business (amended) and Law on Housing (amended). These new laws are scheduled to be adopted by the National Assembly by the end of 2023. It is expected that the new laws will help to speed up the process of land clearance and granting licences for developing real estate projects, creating more products for the real estate market and creating a more transparent, favourable and sustainable real estate market.

17.4 New PDP8 and Energy Transition

[526] With Vietnam's pledge to achieve net-zero carbon emissions by 2050 and the global energy transition, Vietnam's power sector is on the cusp of significant change. Key developments have occurred in recent months, including the adoption of the USD15.5 bn Just Energy Transition Partnership (JETP) with the International Partners Group (IPG) in December 2022 and the issuance of the National Power Development Plan for the period of 2021–2030, with a vision to 2050 (PDP8) in May 2023. PDP8 is largely a strategic document, setting out key aspects and milestones for the development of Vietnam's power sector.

[527] PDP8 projects that Vietnam's electricity demand will continue growing in line with strong GDP growth, reaching 567 bn kWh by 2030 (and about 1 300 bn kWh by 2045). To meet this demand, the country's total installed capacity will increase to about 150 000 MW in 2030 (and around 500 000 GW in 2050).

Transition to greener energy

[528] Coal power, which currently accounts for 34% of electricity generation in Vietnam, will peak by 2030 and be reduced to zero by 2050. Renewables will increase their share of electricity generation, from 25% in 2020 to a baseline of 31% in 2030 and 68% in 2050.

[529] Of renewable sources, the growth of utility-scale solar is expected to be limited in the short term, given the already rapid expansion in the past few years. In contrast, priority will be given to rooftop solar, onshore wind (in the medium term) and offshore wind (in the longer term).

Gas as transition fuel

[530] PDP8 provided governmental investment approvals for a range of new projects, emphasising the usage of domestic gas instead of LNG. This will be the immediate focus of energy developers and the government as energy supply ramps up to provide base load capacity as a substitute for coal-fired power from 9 GW in 2020 to the 37.33 GW expected in 2030. In the longer term, these gas plants should be converted to hydrogen once the technology is commercialised and costs are reduced.

Implementation requires capital

[531] The estimated investment needed by 2030 to achieve the 2030 targets is about USD135 bn, with about 89% of this geared towards the development of energy sources. A further USD400 bn to USD500 bn will be required to achieve the 2050 goals. Foreign capital (including utilisation of the JETP) will be required.

[532] Meanwhile, Electricity of Vietnam, the country's state-owned electric utility, which provides the majority of power to residential, commercial, and industrial customers in the country, was reported to have incurred losses for 2022 and 2023 of nearly USD4 bn. Electricity has been a priority area where the government wants the private sector to play a bigger role. This is because electricity generation is very capital-intensive, and the market can be an efficient way of raising money to finance large-scale investments. This means that foreign investment and international commercial financing will be inevitable in the power sector.

Activities

[533] A number of larger Vietnamese companies that focus on renewable energy include Trung Nam Group, with about 1 500 megawatts, followed by Xuan Thien Group, with nearly 1 200 megawatts, BCG Group, with nearly 600 kilowatts and TTC Group, with more than 400 kilowatts; Gia Lai Electricity Joint Stock Company owns and operates fourteen hydropower plants with the total capacity of 85.1 megawatts and nine solar power farms with the total capacity of 259.4 megawatts.

www.ingramcontent.com/pod-product-compliance
Lightning Source LLC
LaVergne TN
LVHW021037011026
849160LV00009BA/678
9789403545370